COBRA IN THE BOAT
Michael Sata's Zambia

Adonis & Abbey Publishers Ltd
St James House
13 Kensington Square,
London, W8 5HD
United Kingdom

Website: http://www.adonis-abbey.com
E-mail Address: editor@adonis-abbey.com

Nigeria:
Suites C4 & C5 J-Plus Plaza
Asokoro, Abuja, Nigeria
Tel: +234 (0) 7058078841/08052035034

Copyright 2017 © Chisanga Puta-Chekwe

British Library Cataloguing-in-Publication Data
A catalogue record for this book is available from the British
Library

ISBN: 978-1-909112-70-4

COBRA IN THE BOAT
Michael Sata's Zambia

Chisanga Puta-Chekwe

ADONIS & ABBEY
PUBLISHERS LTD

DEDICATION

This book is dedicated to the memory of my ancestor
Mbemba Nshinga (aka Nzinga) c.1456 to 1543; and all family
ancestors who shaped our lives.

Table of Contents

DEDICATION...iv

FOREWORD..vii

INTRODUCTION..xi

PART ONE: It's the Constitution!

CHAPTER ONE
Exploiting a Bad Constitution..17

CHAPTER TWO
Abuse of Parliament by the Executive Branch............................27

CHAPTER THREE
The Vice Presidency...33

CHAPTER FOUR
Dual Citizenship...39

PART TWO: Anaemic Leadership

CHAPTER FIVE
A Foreman in Charge...57

CHAPTER SIX
Bad Decisions...69

CHAPTER SEVEN
Invisible Leadership...73

CHAPTER EIGHT
Unforced Errors..85

CHAPTER NINE
Friends and Allies...99

CHAPTER TEN
Not so Allergic to Corruption..129

CHAPTER ELEVEN
The Essence of Michael Sata..167

Part Three: The Legacy

CHAPTER TWELVE
Man of Action no More...171

CHAPTER THIRTEEN
The Economy Waiting to be created...177

CHAPTER FOURTEEN
Sata's Achievements..223

Index 245

Foreword

Written in a refreshing and easy to read style, "Cobra in the Boat: Michael Sata's Zambia" is perhaps one of the best books written by an indigenous Zambian author on the recent political-economic history of the country. The book examines some of Zambia's public policy positions under President Michael Sata, including issues such as dual citizenship and public finances and expenditure, as well as Sata's often unpredictable political leadership style. The author, Chisanga Puta-Chekwe, a highly accomplished and widely travelled Rhodes Scholar and Oxford graduate, examines Zambia's political-economic history through the prism of the tumultuous political leadership of one Michael Chilufya Sata who served as Zambia's fifth president.

Puta-Chekwe, a former human rights lawyer once incarcerated as a political prisoner in Zambia under the one-party state system of President Kenneth Kaunda, and who later became a very successful business executive in Zambia, the United Kingdom and Canada, brings out in this book a captivating and insightful analysis of the presidency of one of Zambia's former heads of state. Puta-Chekwe knew the late Mr. Sata well. And so, this book is written from both an inside and outside perspective. The book is a candid examination of both the strengths and weaknesses of the man popularly known as, "King Cobra", because of his sharp and insidious tongue.

There is perhaps no better piece of writing on Zambia's President Michael Sata than this book. Puta-Chekwe weaves together intelligently information on the experiences pertaining to the life and political leadership of Sata, capturing also related anecdotes on other political players on Zambia's political landscape, and how, jointly or individually, they influenced the politics of the country. According to Puta-Chekwe, Sata will be judged by what he did, did not do, and how he behaved. Puta-Chekwe adds that Sata was a man of contradictions, and was generally a poor listener who nonetheless sought advice from the most unlikely people, and took action on the basis of that advice.

Puta-Chekwe chronicles Sata's ascendancy to the presidency, pointing out that Sata's tenure as mayor (*i.e.* 'governor', in the *One-Party State* parlance) of Lusaka was characterized by decisive leadership and financial prudence, but that, as president, he was impulsive and profligate as evidenced by his decision to create new districts and a province without proper governmental consultation. On the brighter side though, as Puta-Chekwe observes, according to Zambia's Auditor-General there was a significant drop in the amount of misappropriated public money after Sata took office. Prior to that, in 2010 and 2011, respectively, when the Movement for Multi-Party Democracy (MMD) was in power, approximately US$200,000 was reportedly misappropriated in each of those years. By contrast, a year later, in 2012, that is, the first year after Sata came to power, only US$92,600 was reported as stolen from national coffers.

Be that as it may, the erratic public expenditures incurred during the Sata years were spent mainly on such populist projects as unbudgeted pay increases for low-income Zambians and unjustified pay increases and perquisites for already privileged government officials. According to Puta-Chekwe, Sata was often impatient with theory, but enjoyed the written word.

Puta-Chekwe explains thoughtfully how the people of Zambia appreciated Sata for his work as the mayor of Lusaka and as an effective cabinet minister of the health and local government ministries. But when it came to the presidency, as

Puta-Chekwe observes, the people were reluctant to trust him because of concerns about his perceived unpredictability, lack of diplomacy and impatience. Sata, it is argued, did not come across as a chief executive officer, but rather as a 'foreman' more comfortable with operations than strategy. For three years, Zambia was led by a man who was tempestuous but too ill to always enforce his will. He often got annoyed when people kept him waiting, and stuck relentlessly to routine and protocol when he was well enough to do so.

According to Puta-Chekwe, former US President George Bush's visit to Zambia in July 2012 illustrates the point regarding Sata's lack of diplomacy. Mr. Bush was in the country with his wife, Laura, to promote the work of their cervical cancer prevention foundation, and paid a courtesy call on President Sata at State House. Unfortunately, the Bushes arrived 15 minutes late. Sata was not amused. He complained about the former US president being late for the meeting, adding that were it not for the former 'first couple' bringing money to Zambia, he would not have waited for them. He also dismissed the Bushes' philanthropic work as no more than 'payback time for colonialists.' Sata went on to accuse the United States of abandoning Africa after taking the continent's raw materials to build American cities.

Puta-Chekwe observes that during that incident, Mr. Bush's polite rejoinder that his country never colonized anyone fell on deaf ears, with the Zambian leader firing back that the United States' role in the transatlantic slave industry made them as culpable as European colonial powers. According to Puta-Chekwe, Sata's overreaction to the Bushes' tardiness must be seen from the point of view of a Zambian nationalist acutely aware of the casual and disrespectful manner in which African countries are often treated by American and European media. Puta-Chekwe, who knew Sata personally, writes to explain how on at least one occasion Sata complained to him about 'imperialist' hubris and lack of respect, referring to what Sata saw as the unfair condemnation by the West of anything that Mr. Robert Mugabe, the Zimbabwean president, did. Sata's temperament, as Puta-Chekwe notes, is as much a part of his legacy as the decisions and actions that he took while in office.

No doubt, this book is a timely, well-argued and concisely written narrative. Puta-Chekwe writes with such clarity that readers from all walks of life will find the book a valuable read. Indeed, this is a book that will be useful to many a scholar and reader from different disciplinary backgrounds as well as people from different geographical regions. Puta-Chekwe should be commended for bringing out such an excellent work. I would strongly recommend this book to anyone interested in understanding not only the presidency of Michael Sata but also Zambia's recent political-economic history.

Professor Kenneth Kaoma Mwenda, Senior Counsel in the Legal Vice Presidency of the World Bank in Washington. He is also Adjunct Professor of Law at American University Washington College of Law.

INTRODUCTION

Michael Chilufya Sata was elected president of Zambia after an election widely reported to be the most democratic poll in the country's history. Between 2001 (when he walked out of the ruling MMD party) and September 23, 2011, Sata and his PF party had been in opposition with little prospect (in the eyes of many) of ever forming a government.

Unlike Kenneth Kaunda and Frederick Chiluba, Sata did not come to power as a result of general discontent with the status quo. Unlike Levy Patrick Mwanawasa, Sata was not handpicked to succeed a president constitutionally barred from running for a third term. Sata worked exceptionally hard to earn his victory against great odds. He was only the second person in the republic's history to defeat a sitting president.

His campaign symbol, a boat, promised speedy deliverance from Zambia's woes. But the wind was not always with the boat and it turned out that winning the election of 2011 was the easy part. The many years in opposition combined with Sata's personality led his Patriotic Front Party to make campaign promises that proved incapable of eventual fulfilment while in office. Of course most reasonable people knew that the more extravagant promises made during the hustings could not be fulfilled, but these people also believed that a PF government would nonetheless bring about the expected change. Problems like inadequate housing for low income Zambians and the crafting of a viable constitution for the republic that had been allowed to fester, would be addressed and in some instances the solution would appear within 90 days of taking power, as promised by the populist leader.

Though few rational thinkers believed housing problems could be solved within this time frame, many others believed that the constitutional issue would at last be resolved within the shortest possible time. This is because numerous constitutional reviews and commissions over the years had highlighted issues of most concern to Zambians that the nation clearly wished could be incorporated into the fundamental law of the land. These issues included the 50 + one formula for electing presidents; a legislature independent of the executive branch; dual citizenship for Zambians; a more independent judiciary and a more independent public service including the police service.

The PF campaign did not disappoint. It promised all this as the way forward. The Boat or '*Ubwato*' in the local language was indeed the appropriate vehicle for moving forward.

Expectations were high and there was confidence in the view that the PF would be a government of action and that action would commence from the first day of the new administration's term of office.

But the PF had been in opposition for a decade; become comfortable with opposition politics, and paid little attention to the realities of government and issues of governance. The party did not adequately prepare for office. For this reason there was less action than one would have expected, and many unforced errors during the Sata years.

The PF leader had alienated himself from the ruling MMD government in which he held many positions including the office of minister without portfolio. Indeed he had served as secretary general of the party he now despised. He left the MMD government principally because President Frederick Chiluba had failed to endorse him as successor, choosing instead the more level headed Mwanawasa who it was presumed would be more accommodating and protective of Chiluba once the latter left office.

Sata's obstinate character did not allow him to emulate anything from the party he now despised. When he got to power therefore, he was reluctant to use the MMD government as the starting reference point; instead he went back in time to the days of the United National Independence Party (UNIP) and used those days as his main point of reference. Sata's sudden rapprochement with UNIP was ironic as he was among a group of former UNIP government officials who had resigned from UNIP in early 1991 to form the Movement for Multiparty Democracy, on the ground that the UNIP government had undermined individual freedom and destroyed the economy.

It mattered not to Mr. Sata that the UNIP model, if one could call it that, was largely irrelevant to contemporary 2011 Zambian society. Not only had the world changed but Zambia specifically had changed and would now be intolerant of a government as dictatorial and economically innocent as the UNIP government had been. The world now has less sympathy for dictatorship to the extent that there is now an international criminal court that will not hesitate to indict and try leaders accused of gross misrule.

Despite this reality Mr. Sata forged a public and mutually beneficial alliance with Mr. Kaunda. That was the first major indicator of how Mr. Sata was going to rule. Why did Sata find this alliance necessary? The answer given by many PF officials (embarrassed by this alliance) is that Mr. Sata simply wanted to give due recognition to Mr. Kaunda as first president of the republic. The real answer may be more complex and may involve the fact that both Mr. Kaunda and Mr. Sata had a common political enemy in Frederick Chiluba, the founding president of the MMD. Chiluba denied Sata a chance to become president. He also ended Kaunda's presidency, much to the former president's chagrin.

Both Kaunda and Sata were comfortable placing populism ahead of sound economic policy. The consequences of today's populism have been economically deleterious but in more democratic Zambia it may be possible to reverse more quickly some of this harm than it was in the immediate aftermath of Mr. Kaunda's rule. Kaunda's legacy is dominated by conversion of Zambia into a politically intolerant one party state, acute shortages of food, and routine imprisonment and torture of perceived political enemies.

It is difficult to see a replay of this calamity. Consequently, PF populism may not be as deleterious as Mr. Kaunda's dictatorship. Nevertheless the Sata years, characterised by Sata's illness, erratic decision making, a casual attitude toward currency and foreign exchange regime management, and political intolerance, will have some impact on Zambia's development. This impact will however be mitigated by Sata's steadfast commitment to Zambian sovereignty, infrastructure development, gender equality, and also by the seemingly irreversible reforms of the 1990s.

Part One
It's the Constitution!

CHAPTER ONE

Exploiting a Bad Constitution

Historically, Zambian constitutions have been drafted and amended under the guidance of the executive branch with a view to serving the interests of a political clique in the community but not necessarily the entire country. As leader of the Patriotic Front Party in opposition, Mr. Michael Chilufya Sata recognised this fact. He considered the enactment of a more equitable constitution an absolute priority, going so far as to declare that the new fundamental law of the land had to be in place before the general election scheduled to take place in 2011. This declaration was made in March 2007, more than four years before Mr. Sata and the Patriotic Front came to power.

The future president promised a sustained campaign to ensure that a new constitution was in place before 2011. According to the March 10, 2007 edition of *the Post* Mr. Sata believed that the then incumbent president, Levy Mwanawasa was terrified of enacting the kind of constitution Zambians clearly wanted because he knew this would lead to the demise of the ruling MMD party. Although *the Post* did not make the connection at that time, Sata was calling specifically for the adoption of what has come to be known as the *50 plus one* clause. This clause makes it mandatory to have a runoff election between the two top candidates in the event of no candidate securing more than 50 per cent of the vote in the first round of the poll.

Sata once again was in tune with the thinking of the general public. His analysis that the Zambian Constitution in its current form was defective was quite right. Other opposition leaders notably Mr. Hakainde Hichilema of the United Party for National Development stood with Sata on this point.

Before discussing the apparent U turn made by the Patriotic Front government on this point after it came to power, it is important to give a brief history of constitutional development in modern Zambia.

The pre-independence constitution, under which the 1962 general election was contested, was designed to minimise the likelihood of the nationalist parties winning power outright. That constitution thus gave disproportional electoral power to the white settler community.

The 1964 constitution had broader participation in its formulation than its predecessor, but even this document was not truly a creation of the Zambian people as it was negotiated by the British government, the nationalist leadership, and representatives of the white settler community. The public at large was not meaningfully engaged. The constitution did nevertheless protect basic human rights and define structures and powers of government.

The 1972 constitution served an even smaller base of stakeholders than its predecessors because its sole purpose was to preserve the power of the United National Independence Party and its leader Kenneth Kaunda. There was no opportunity for the Zambian public to oppose the establishment of a one party state (merely to suggest the form it should take) and this fact undermined the legitimacy of the nationwide consultation exercise that preceded the creation of the Second Republic.

The 1991 constitution was a product of the Constitution Commission of Inquiry appointed in 1990 under the leadership of Professor Patrick Mvunga. The 1991 document reintroduced political pluralism and ushered in the Third Republic. Although the ratification of the constitution was preceded by an inquiry, the urgent political circumstances of the day were such that no comprehensive and all-encompassing discussion could take place. UNIP's rule had become untenable but there was no lawful manner within the existing constitution of retiring the autocratic government. A new dispensation was needed immediately. Despite the tight timeframe within which a new basic law of governance had to be produced, the Mvunga constitution reversed some of the losses made during the one-party era. Indeed this is the constitution that made it possible for the then opposition Movement for Multiparty Democracy to legally contest the 1991 presidential and parliamentary elections.

Although Professor Mvunga is better known as an academic lawyer, at the time he chaired the Commission of Inquiry, he was serving as Zambia's solicitor general and was thus a member of the executive branch of government. It is typical for the executive branch to seek to control the constitution making process, and the branch usually does this by ensuring that one of its representatives heads the commission of inquiry. This pattern was relaxed however after MMD came to power and appears to have been abandoned altogether by the Mwanawasa government.

Before coming to power, the MMD had undertaken to change the hastily drafted 1991 Constitution and replace it with a new dispensation preceded by a process that was more inclusive and less partisan than hitherto. Thus on 22 December 1993, the new Zambian president asked the respected lawyer John Mupanga Mwanakatwe to head what came to be known as the Mwanakatwe Constitutional Review Commission. Mwanakatwe had previously served as Minister of Education and Minister of Finance in the first and second republics. At the time of his appointment however he was not a member of the government but a well-established member of the private sector practising law in the Zambian capital.

The Mwanakatwe Commission had broadly defined terms of reference that included recommending a system that would ensure that Zambia was governed in a manner that promoted the democratic principles of regular and fair elections, transparency and accountability, and that would guard against the re-emergence of a dictatorial form of government.

The Commission undertook an extensive tour of the country soliciting views from the citizenry. The citizens did not disappoint and expressed their views without restraint as befitting a recently emancipated people. There was overwhelming support for the view that a presidential candidate must receive 50 per cent plus one of the votes cast, for him or her to be declared a winner. The population also seemed to favour adoption of the new constitution by way of a constituent assembly attended by representatives of all political parties, civil society, trade unions, women's groups, churches and many others, the *raison d'être* being that this would ensure maximum participation in the constitution making process by Zambians and their various stakeholder groups. In addition, the desire that the final document should be approved in a referendum was expressed.

By the time the Mwanakatwe Commission reported, the MMD had been in power for almost five years. The 'new' president and his team were now less keen on transparency than they had been just a few years earlier. The White Paper following the Commission's report rejected the idea of a constituent assembly and a referendum. It also rejected the 50 per cent plus one recommendation with respect to presidential elections. Furthermore, the government declined to consider the introduction of new personal rights and the creation of a constitutional court and a more independent electoral commission.

It should be noted that Michael Chilufya Sata was a member of the MMD government that rejected these important clauses of the draft Mwanakatwe Constitution.

By abandoning its 1991 promise to introduce a constitution that would strengthen individual rights and freedoms, and lessen the powers of the executive branch, the Chiluba government missed an opportunity to remedy Zambia's historic constitutional ills. In contrast, the government was quick to accept the regressive recommendation that a presidential candidate had to be born of parents who were citizens of Zambia by birth. Far from being non-partisan, this provision was aimed at preventing Kenneth Kaunda, who had recently come out of retirement, from contesting the 1996 general election.

Despite expressions of serious concern about the new constitution, Chiluba's government proceeded to give effect to its White Paper by amending every part of the 1991 Constitution save for part III, which governs protection of fundamental rights and freedoms of the individual, and requires a national referendum to be amended.

The stage was thus set for yet another constitutional review commission. Zambians still needed a durable constitution that would allow them to be governed with equity. It is not surprising therefore that less than 18 months after President Chiluba's term of office came to an end, the new Zambian leader, Levy Patrick Mwanawasa, announced the appointment of yet another constitutional review commission. He called upon civil society groups to nominate members to sit on this commission.

The new commission was led by a British-trained lawyer who had previously served as president of the African

Development Bank. Although Willa Mung'omba had been a member of parliament in the 1970s, he had never served in the executive branch of government.

In her essay on *Discrimination and the Law pertaining to Immigration*, Susan Margaret Clayton has suggested that "Mung'omba [was] the first chair of a constitutional review process that had not been in the executive or under executive direction, which may lend a measure of independence and therefore credibility to his commission."

Like the Mwanakatwe inquiry, the Mung'omba Commission toured the country extensively, and obtained a wide range of views from people. Its interim report and draft constitution were presented in 2005.

It is noteworthy that the Commission recommended adoption of the draft constitution by a constituent assembly and thereafter approval by the general population in a referendum. Like the Mwanakatwe Commission and in keeping with the wishes of most of civil society, the Mung'omba exercise also recommended that a successful presidential candidate should obtain 50 per cent plus one of the votes cast, in order to be elected. In the event of none of the candidates meeting this threshold, there should be a runoff between the two frontrunners.

The government of the day appeared reluctant to establish a constituent assembly and never missed the opportunity to remind interlocutors on the matter that the Constitution of Zambia clearly stated that the legislative power of the Republic of Zambia was vested solely in parliament, and it did not provide for adoption of constitutional amendments by a constituent assembly.

With respect to the 50 per cent plus one recommendation, the government justified rejection of the clause on the ground that electoral reruns are costly and add to uncertainty.

But the National Constitutional Conference established by the Mwanawasa government to discuss the Mung'omba Commission recommendations also proved to be an expensive venture not least because of the lavish allowances given to members and witnesses (who appeared in no hurry to conclude their business.) According to the *Zambian Economist* edition of 18 December 2007, the National Constitutional Conference delegates were entitled to a sitting allowance of US $104 per session and a daily subsistence allowance US $135. In addition to that they were also entitled to a transport allowance of US $20 per day if they resided in Lusaka and US$62.50 if they lived outside the capital region. Thus a Lusaka based delegate could expect to be paid US$ 259 a day. By way of contrast Zambian nurses at the time earned an average monthly salary of US$ 229 or US7.60 a day, according to the *Medicus Mundi Schweiz Bulletin* of May 2007. (It may also be useful to point out that the daily subsistence allowance for public officials working away from base in Ontario at that time was less than $50.)

Advocates of a constituent assembly only had to point to this extravagance to rebut claims that their preferred method of adopting the new constitution was unaffordable.

Nevertheless the Mwanawasa approach was more promising than his predecessors' had been. But the Mwanawasa promise did not lead to a new constitution and both the presidential by election of 2008 made necessary by Mwanawasa's death, and the scheduled 2011 poll were contested under the 1996 constitution.

In accordance with that constitution, the Zambia Electoral Commission reported on September 23, 2011 that Sata's Patriotic Front had won 43% of votes cast in the poll against incumbent Banda's 36%. The other way of framing the result is that the opposition parties obtained 57% of the vote compared to the PF's 43%. Had the draft constitution been in effect, a second round of voting would have been necessary and it is not inconceivable that President Rupiah Banda as the runner up candidate would have persuaded the United Party for National Development and the smaller National Restoration Party (NAREP) to back him, and keep Sata out of the State House.

The PF government was aware of this reality and until late 2015 took the view (privately) that its chances of success in the next scheduled general and presidential election in 2016 were enhanced by the 1996 constitution, and possibly dimmed by the draft one. This is why Mr. Sata and his government were in no hurry to implement the draft constitution.

The main opposition MMD party has spent much of its time since losing office regretting its refusal to abandon the 1996 constitution in favour of a more equitable fundamental law. On January 7, 2014, *the Post* newspaper reported that the level headed MMD Vice President for political affairs, Mr. Michael Kaingu had admitted that his party had failed the Zambian people over the constitution-making process.

Mr. Kaingu now called upon the ruling PF party "to correct the mistake committed" by MMD and enact the draft constitution before the 2016 elections. In effect Kaingu created an opening for productive dialogue over the constitution with the government. Unfortunately Kaingu's interlocutor on this occasion, the Chief Government Spokesperson and Minister of Information Mwansa Kapeya, completely missed the opportunity and instead resorted to vituperative and unproductive dialogue that was the hallmark of his government. Mr. Kapeya's response to Kaingu was to castigate him for what he termed "hypocrisy".

The Honourable Minister found it "laughable" that Kaingu would have the temerity to demand a new constitution in short order when Kaingu's party when in government had itself missed the opportunity to scrap the 1996 constitution and replace it with the draft Mung'omba Constitution.

Mr. Kapeya's argument missed the point. It was Kapeya's party while in opposition that had repeatedly promised a new constitution within 90 days of being elected. More than two years after assuming power, that constitution was still not in place. Kaingu had the right as a citizen of Zambia to enquire about his government's failure to deliver on this specific and important promise.

Mr. Kapeya's response contrasted markedly with the approach taken only one day earlier by Mrs. Inonge Wina then gender and child development minister and national chairperson of the PF party.

Mrs. Wina was categorical that her government had not reneged on its promise to deliver a people-driven constitution. Her interlocutor was Mutale Nalumango, chairperson of the UPND and former MMD Member of Parliament. Unlike Mr. Kapeya, Ms. Wina not only acknowledged the promise made by her party over the constitution but she also sought to explain why the implementation of the new fundamental law had been delayed. Her explanation was brave but unconvincing. According to Mrs. Wina a constitution is too important a national document to be drafted and implemented without consensus.

The fact is however consensus on the kind of constitution Zambia should have was reached a long time ago. It was indeed the PF's argument while in opposition that the basic elements of the constitution had been agreed upon by the Zambian population and because of this a new constitution could be implemented within 90 days of the PF taking power.

It is doubtful Mrs. Wina believed that the new constitution would be delivered any time soon and perhaps the best evidence for this is the fact that she took the earliest opportunity in her response to Ms. Nalumango to change the subject.

The 1996 constitution was convenient for any government that did not enjoy the support of a majority of the nation because it made possible the election of a minority government.

In light of this, Edgar Lungu who succeeded Michael Sata as both PF party and republican president deserves huge praise for persuading his party (and parliament) to adopt the 50 plus one clause. President Lungu appended his signature to Constitution Bill Number 17 of 2015 on January 05, 2016 and thereby brought to an end one of the country's most contentious constitutional debates.

Henceforth the Zambian president will lose the power to hire and fire vice presidents at will. The new constitution requires all presidential candidates to declare an official running mate when they submit their nomination papers. That running mate goes on to become vice president in the event of the ticket succeeding at the polls.

President Lungu was not unaware of the potential consequences of this change. He was clear in his speech at the signing ceremony that the effect of the amendment would be to reduce presidential power. The amendment would also make it impossible for any political party to win power without the support of the majority of voters. That must be a good thing for democracy.

CHAPTER TWO

Abuse of Parliament by the Executive Branch

By clinging to the out-dated 1996 constitution, President Sata also missed the opportunity to end historic abuse of the legislature by successive governments.

The 1996 constitution limits the president's choice when he or she is appointing members of the executive branch by requiring members of cabinet to also be members of the legislature. Thus Zambia does not have a clear separation of powers between the legislative and executive branches of government. Experience shows that the integration of these two branches of government has not aided the objectives of good governance in Zambia and has from time to time undermined democracy.

All too often the government has dominated the legislative branch so much as to effectively render it ineffective as an instrument of democratic oversight.

When the PF won the general election in 2011 it secured 60 out of the 148 contested seats. President Sata then exercised his right under the constitution to appoint eight unelected members. In his haste Mr. Sata actually announced the appointment of more members than he was allowed to but subsequently dropped some names in order to comply with the provisions of the constitution.

This gave the PF 68 members. After two by elections, the PF added two more members to their contingent for a total of 70 MPs.

This was not, evidently, enough to stop the ruling party from continuing the hunt for new MPs to bolster its position in parliament. In fact the PF was so aggressive in this endeavour that in July 2012 Movement for Multiparty

Democracy (MMD) president, Nevers Mumba, announced that all MMD members of parliament who had accepted positions in President Michael Sata's government should either relinquish their ministerial posts or face expulsion from the MMD. Of the nine MMD MPs serving in the PF government, only one, Deputy Minister of Mines Isaac Banda, followed the directive.

Mumba was irked because he and fellow leaders of the MMD had not been consulted when the appointments were made. Sata and the PF, on the other hand, justified the appointments of the MPs on the basis of national inclusion. Both the PF and MMD were being disingenuous.

As the Zambian political commentator Sishuwa D Sishuwa pointed out in a lucid piece in *the Post* newspaper on July 29, 2012, the practice of 'poaching' opposition MPs was started by the MMD in 2002 when President Levy Mwanawasa offered cabinet and deputy ministerial positions to opposition MPs in order to bolster MMD numbers in parliament and make it easier for the government to pass legislation.

Thus Sylvia Masebo (from the Zambia Republican Party) Dipak Patel, Geoffrey Samukonga and Chance Kabaghe (from the Forum for Democracy and Development) Jonas Shakafuswa (from the United Party for National Development) Gladys Nyirongo, Patrick Musonda, Ronald Banda and Nedson Nzowa (from the Heritage Party) and Chile Ng'uni (from the United National Independence Party), were all given jobs in the executive branch of government.

These appointments were made unilaterally without consultation with the parties to which the opposition MPs belonged.

In May 2003, Mr. Nevers Mumba himself had succumbed to the temptation of high office when President Mwanawasa offered him the republican vice presidency. Mr. Mumba was required to dissolve his party, the National Citizens Coalition, as a condition of the offer. In similar fashion Dr. Inonge Mbikusita-Lewanika disbanded her party, Agenda for Zambia, in return for an ambassadorship in Washington.

At the time, Mwanawasa came under pressure from civil society and opposition parties who accused him of trying to weaken and manipulate the opposition.

But this practice was not confined to Mwanawasa's MMD. Rupiah Banda who succeeded Mwanawasa in 2008, appointed UNIP's Mkhondo Lungu as Minister of Home Affairs and the PF's Besa Chimbaka as provincial minister for the Luapula Province.

So both the MMD and the PF have been guilty of the practice of co-opting opposition parliamentarians for the purpose of strengthening executive power in the legislature. They have done so simply because the 1996 constitution allowed them to. Unfortunately the end result of the practice has been to weaken parliament and undermine its ability to check the executive branch.

The strong presence of the executive in the legislature encourages ruling party members of parliament, and even some opposition members, to seize every opportunity to support the government in the hope that such support will be favourably noticed by the government and lead to reward in the form of ministerial or other appointment. Conversely, criticism of the government, however legitimate, is avoided. In the circumstances only opposition Members of Parliament uninterested in government appointment can be relied upon for routine criticism of the government.

This gratuitous support for the government has allowed all post-independence governments to use the legislature as a rubber stamp, and harmed democracy.

But the executive branch is also harmed by the absence of a clear separation of powers. Save for the eight nominated members, parliamentarians are elected by constituencies. Although there is a certain amount of political sophistication and respect for ideology in urban constituencies of the Copperbelt Province, the same cannot always be said for rural and semi-rural areas. In order to win in these constituencies, candidates must not only be well versed in local issues, they must also identify emotionally and ethnically with the area.

A good example of this arose during the campaign for the parliamentary by election in the Katuba constituency when UPND leader Hakainde Hichilema urged people in the area not to vote for the PF candidate Moses Chilando because he allegedly came from another region of the country.

Mr. Chilando was in fact a local resident who spoke the local Lenje language. His crime in the eyes of the UPND leader was that he was an ethnic Bemba. As *the Post* newspaper reported on February 23, 2014, Mr. Hakainde was not alone in holding this view. The local headman Mupwaya Agrippa Phiri was even more explicit when he described the UPND as a political party for the Bantu Botatwe ethnic grouping of Tonga, Lenje and Ila Zambians. Mr. Hakainde Hichilema did not contradict this opinion.

While the headman's utterances had limited impact, the fact that a leader of a national party would discriminate so overtly against other Zambians led many to question Mr. Hichilema's suitability for any kind of national office.

It is not difficult to imagine that the UPND candidate who went on to win the election by a comfortable margin of 2034 votes over Mr. Chilando who polled 2747 votes, would see himself as a representative not only of his particular constituency but more generally as an advocate of the Bantu

Botatwe grouping. He would apparently do all this with the sanction of his leader!

But the results also show that the people of Katuba have not given up on the idea of a united Zambia. Mr. Chilando, who was depicted as an alien by the UPND, got 2747 votes. That was a respectable showing given the naked bigotry of the UPND and also in light of the intimidation and violence that occurred on polling day.

Often the issues in rural and semi-rural areas are unique and sometimes different from national issues. A person elected in one of these constituencies and subsequently elevated to the cabinet will often find it difficult to reconcile local and national interests.

This conflict often leads to the parliamentarian seeing him or herself as 'the people's champion' in cabinet. Many ethnic tensions, typically provoked by a development project being placed in one part of the country rather than another, have their roots in this reality. A clear separation of powers would avoid this problem by allowing the president to appoint to the cabinet any citizen unencumbered by ethnicity, as long as that person was not a parliamentarian, member of the judiciary, civil servant, or otherwise legally barred from serving.

The Sata administration did nothing to rectify this constitutional defect. Even President Lungu (who proved to be more progressive than Michael Sata) failed to champion the separation of powers clause in the draft Mung'omba constitution. Thus the constitutional amendment signed by President Lungu at the beginning of 2016 did not contain this clause.

CHAPTER THREE

The Vice Presidency

Far from addressing the country's constitutional challenges, the Sata government sometimes compounded the problem. The issue of the vice presidency is a case in point.

Following the victory of the Patriotic Front in the 2011 general election, the newly installed President Sata moved quickly to appoint his long time lieutenant, Guy Scott (who had also won his own Lusaka Central parliamentary seat in the general election) as Zambia's Vice President.

Scott's appointment was made pursuant to Article 45 (1) of the Zambian constitution which created the office of vice-president of the republic. The Constitution further empowered the President to appoint from "amongst the members of the National Assembly" a vice-president.

Ordinarily the Vice President acts for the president whenever the latter is out of the country or is otherwise unable to discharge his or her duties. But Guy Scott was no ordinary vice president.

Born in 1944 in the southern Zambian resort town of Livingstone to British immigrants, Alec and Grace Scott, Guy Scott completed his education in Southern Rhodesia (now Zimbabwe) and the United Kingdom.

After graduating from Cambridge University in 1965 he joined the Government of the Republic of Zambia where he served as a planner in the Ministry of Finance. At the same time he served as deputy editor of the magazine *Business and Economy of East and Central Africa*.

Five years after joining the public service, he left to try his hand in the private sector. He started a farming venture that concentrated on non-traditional crops like irrigated wheat and strawberries.

Later, Walkover Estate, as the agro-business was known, joined forces with the Commonwealth Development Corporation to found the Mpongwe Development Company in the Copperbelt Province of Zambia.

The company, established on thousands of acres of dry bush using large scale irrigation with great success, was soon hailed as a model of development, able to produce, according to Geoff Tyler the CDC's former representative in Zambia, "50% of Zambia's soya crop, 40% of its wheat and was the largest single source of maize in the country."

Mr. Scott thus showed some success in agriculture and it would soon be time for him to show his mettle in politics.

By 1990 it was evident that Kaunda's One Party State was vulnerable and possibly on its last legs. A pressure group known as the Movement for Multi-Party Democracy started a vigorous campaign across the country to peacefully persuade the authorities to reintroduce democracy. The group achieved its aim within a year and transformed itself into a political party.

Scott was an early member of the Movement for Multi-Party Democracy and was elected to serve as chair of the agriculture committee at the Party's first convention.

On October 31, 1991 Zambia went to the polls with Guy Scott as the parliamentary candidate for the MMD in Mpika, a largely rural constituency in northern Zambia. He easily won the seat. Scott was subsequently appointed Minister of Agriculture, Food and Fisheries. He presided over a number of policy reforms and was responsible for managing the "drought of the century" in January and February 1992. One of Scott's infamous decisions was to abolish the National Marketing Board (NAMBOARD). The organisation was far from perfect but one of the things it did well was to distribute seed and fertilizer on credit to small scale farmers across the country, in addition to buying their produce. The decision to abolish NAMBOARD without finding an alternative method of supporting small scale farmers was disastrous in a country where the majority of the staple crop is produced by peasant farmers with limited resources. It also made a mockery of Scott's plan to stimulate agricultural output. Citing the World Bank, Andrew Sardanis has recorded that this decision resulted in 60-70 per cent of small scale farmers being excluded from participation in the plan (*Zambia: The First 50 years p.130*).

In 1996, Scott resigned from the MMD to form the Lima Party with Ben Kapita, the then-president of the Zambia National Farmers Union. Despite attempts to merge with other parties, Lima was not a great political success. That failure did not however dampen Scott's enthusiasm for politics. In 2001, he joined the newly formed Patriotic Front, subsequently winning a parliamentary seat in the capital city and thus returning to the National Assembly.

All this, and his relatively high level of cultural literacy, would appear to make Guy Scott not only a plausible candidate for the vice presidency but the presidency itself.

Not so in Zambia. A candidate for the office of president must not only be a Zambian citizen; his or her parents must also be Zambian citizens by birth or descent. It will be recalled that Guy Scott's parents, Alec and Grace, arrived in Zambia or Northern Rhodesia as it then was, in 1927 and 1940 respectively. Alec and Grace were not Zambians either by birth or descent.

On the face of it therefore Guy Scott would appear to be barred by the 1996 constitution from serving as president.

It is perhaps for this reason that President Sata consistently by passed Guy Scott when picking a cabinet minister to act on his behalf whenever he travelled abroad.

This unnecessary arrangement caused confusion. On the one hand Mr. Sata was happy to appoint Guy Scott vice president but on the other he did not allow him to fulfill an essential responsibility of the vice presidency, namely to act for the President when the latter was out of the country.

Mr. Sata could have ended the uncertainty by either not appointing Scott as vice president or seeking a declaratory judgement from the court about Scott's ability to act as president when the head of state was out of the country.

Many legal scholars believe that while a person whose parents were born outside Zambia may not be eligible for election as president, that person could nonetheless serve as acting president. These scholars were proved right when Michael Chilufya Sata died at a private clinic in London on October 28, 2014. After taking the advice of the attorney general, Mr. Edgar Lungu, the acting president, readily handed power over to Guy Scott, the republican vice president. Guy Scott was the vice president and the constitution said the vice president assumed power on an interim basis in the event of the death of the president.

It is worth repeating that had Zambia adopted a constitution that provided for an elected vice president earlier, the nation would have been saved both money and anxiety as the elected vice president would have assumed power automatically without recourse to an expensive special election.

In January 2016, parliament finally amended the constitution in order to provide for an elected vice president.

Guy Scott, Zambia's first white interim President

CHAPTER FOUR

Dual Citizenship

Reflecting the interests of the white settler community that liked the idea of continuing to live in Zambia but that also wanted the protection of British citizenship should the new country fail or be hostile to their community, the 1964 Constitution bestowed citizenship on every person who was a British protected person by virtue of having been born in the former protectorate of Northern Rhodesia before independence. The Constitution also confirmed the citizenship of people born in Zambia after independence. Evidently no feminists were involved in negotiating the 1964 Constitution which denied citizenship to persons born outside Zambia of a Zambian mother and a non-Zambian father.

The 1964 Constitution remained largely unchallenged until 1972 when the political elite decided it could no longer contain the opposition and be assured of success at future elections. The elite thus prepared to turn the country into a one party state. The new thinking was clearly inconsistent with the West European secularist ideas incorporated in the 1964 Constitution.

The advocates of the one party state were increasingly anti-European and xenophobic in their views. It is not surprising that in 1972 Mainza Chona, the head of the National Commission on the Establishment of a 'One Party Participatory Democracy' in Zambia, reported that most petitioners "felt that Zambian citizenship should be acquired through descent only and that citizenship by registration or naturalisation should be discontinued".

In defiance of the principle that birth guarantees citizenship, the Chona Commission also recommended that children of foreigners born in Zambia should only be able to acquire citizenship by way of formal application when they attained the age of majority.

The purpose of this recommendation was to prevent people born in Zambia but with no other connection to or interest in Zambia from becoming citizens.

The One Party Constitution did remove the sexist provision with respect to those born outside Zambia to a non-Zambian father. Now people born outside Zambia could claim their Zambian citizenship if at least one of the parents was a Zambian citizen. This victory for equality was however quickly undermined by another provision that denied Zambian born children citizenship if one of their parents was a non-resident alien and the other a resident. Thus a child born in Zambia to a resident mother and non-resident father could not become a citizen of the republic.

The 1973 Constitution is an example of the folly of limited consultation and too much reliance on the executive branch of government in crafting the country's supreme law. It is also an example of an overly prescriptive constitution. The citizenship provisions inherited from the 1973 constitution are covered in ten lengthy clauses of considerable complexity.

In contrast, this is how the United States Constitution declares citizenship rights:

> All persons born or naturalized in the United States, and subject to the jurisdiction thereof, are citizens of the United States and of the State wherein they reside. No State shall make or enforce any law which shall abridge the privileges or immunities of citizens of the United States; nor shall any State deprive any person of life, liberty, or property, without due process of law; nor deny to any person within its jurisdiction the equal protection of the laws.

The Zambian Constitution continues to permit citizenship by registration although the prescribed period of prior residence has been varied from four years in 1964 to ten years. The longer period of residence is a result of concerns expressed by petitioners who made representations to the Chona Commission. As has been pointed out, the extent to which these petitioners could be said to be representative of the country is doubtful. Even so, their xenophobia continued to be reflected in the constitution and even found its way into the draft Mung'omba Constitution which extended the residency period to twelve years. In the draft Mung'omba Constitution, a foreigner wishing to become a Zambian citizen can either be 'lawfully resident' or 'ordinarily resident' in Zambia for the prescribed period.

The registration provisions in both the 1996 constitution and the Mung'omba draft Constitution ignore the realities of the global economy, apart from being unfair to both the country and the prospective citizen.

Successful countries understand that the challenge of attracting the best human capital is much greater in the new global economy than it has been in the past. With increased mobility of labour the competition between countries to attract the best and the brightest has become fierce. By making it difficult for skilled foreigners to become Zambian citizens, the Zambians in effect told the world that any country could fish in their waters but they weren't going to fish in other countries' waters. In other words Zambia is deliberately limiting its ability to recruit the talent necessary to propel it into the technological era while at the same time being indifferent to losing the talent it already has, to foreign countries.

Many foreigners enter Zambia with a view to doing skilled work or investing in businesses. The foreigners who like

Zambia and contemplate taking out citizenship, have to wait for ten years before they can legally do so. During that ten year wait, they can of course change their minds and perhaps leave the country, taking their skills with them. They certainly will avoid making long term investments, and they will externalise as much of the income they earn in Zambia as possible.

On the other hand, if foreigners were allowed to apply for citizenship after a residency period of four years, as was the case under the 1964 Constitution, the decision to become Zambians would obviously be made earlier leading to other economically beneficial decisions like investing in property from the fifth year onwards. Necessarily the new Zambians would spend most of their money at home, leading to a reduction in the rate of foreign remittances.

The current policy of discouraging foreigners from becoming Zambian citizens as soon as possible continues to be costly to the country. Since independence Zambia has remitted abroad hundreds of millions of dollars on behalf of expatriate labour. That money could have been invested at home, for the benefit of all Zambians.

In contrast, Canadians have no doubt that they benefit from immigration and consequently the vast majority of people landing in the country do so as permanent residents. It only takes three years of continuous residence for a permanent resident to be eligible for Canadian citizenship. There is no shortage of evidence to show that new Canadians invest quickly and significantly in their new country.

Those who favour long periods of residence before foreigners can naturalise and become citizens argue that future Zambians must demonstrate their loyalty to the country and demonstrate to the authorities that they will not bring injurious cultures to Zambia. These are legitimate concerns. Zambia should certainly do all it can to avoid the importation of such social ills as apartheid, racism, and religious fanaticism. The assessment of suitability of would-be citizens and avoidance of undesirable aliens can however be effectively accomplished through appropriately designed citizenship examinations.

The country could again look to Canada in this regard. Canada not only has a points system that qualifies candidates for residency but it also has an examination for residents who wish to take out Canadian citizenship. The United Kingdom has also recently introduced an examination for prospective Britons. This is one way of ensuring that new citizens understand the values of the society they are joining.

In any case foreigners in Zambia are routinely screened by the Ministry of Home Affairs for suitability as residents. It should not be too difficult therefore to assess which of these foreigners have the potential to be good, law abiding and productive Zambian citizens.

One more point about the registration provisions of the constitution. Until 2016 satisfying the residency period was not enough. The foreigner seeking Zambian citizenship could not be considered for registration until he or she attained the age of twenty-one. The age requirement appeared justifiable only in the historic context and had little relevance. The age of majority in Zambia has been eighteen since the early 1970s. Why then was eligibility for citizenship denied to an eighteen year old deemed mature enough to vote, until 2016?

One Citizen, Two Countries

The economic decline of the 1980s and 1990s severely restricted opportunities at home and led many skilled Zambians to seek employment abroad. In 1992 Zambia's veteran foreign affairs minister, Vernon Mwaanga, estimated for example that at the close of the 1980s more than one half of all qualified teachers in secondary schools in Botswana were of Zambian origin. There were also Zambian pharmacists in the United Kingdom, software designers and computer programmers in the United States and Australia, and lawyers, doctors, engineers, and scientists in Canada.

Many urban middle class Zambians now have relations or friends who live permanently abroad. There are also many Zambians born abroad but with familial, historic and cultural links to their country of origin. It should not be a surprise therefore that there is broader support today for dual citizenship than at any time in the history of the young republic.

The prohibition of dual citizenship in the One Party Constitution achieved nothing and succeeded in only further alienating Zambia from the international community. The more enlightened Mung'omba Constitutional Review Commission understood this and recommended that dual citizenship should be allowed for Zambian citizens born to a Zambian parent who is a citizen by birth or descent. Although this constitutes progress, the Mung'omba proposals still did not allow Zambians by registration or naturalisation to enjoy dual nationality.

During the Sata years however the issue was not so much how far the Mung'omba proposals went; rather the issue was an absence of political leadership to advance the agenda on dual citizenship. President Sata was instinctively hostile to the idea of dual citizenship. Apart from Sata's instinctive fear that dual citizenship would somehow undermine the country's sovereignty, the reasons for this hostility were never clear as most of the statements made on the issue by the president lacked policy coherence.

On one occasion he condemned dual citizenship by analogising that one could not be both Lozi and Tonga at the same time. The analogy was both inaccurate and inappropriate. There are many Zambians who have Lozi mothers and Tonga fathers and vice versa and who consider themselves both Lozi and Tonga. Furthermore it was disturbing that the head of state appeared to imply that ethnic divisions in Zambia were unbridgeable. It would have been interesting to ask the President whether it was possible for one to be both Zambian and Lozi!

During a June 2012 visit to London, Mr. Sata met UK based Zambians at the official residence of the Zambian High Commissioner. On that occasion the president again opposed the proposal to amend the Constitution so as to incorporate provisions permitting dual citizenship. In his view amending the law to allow dual citizenship would increase the number of Zambians 'and jobs will be taken away by other nationalities living in the country.'

This implied that Mr. Sata did not want the Zambian population to increase and that there were limited job opportunities in Zambia. And yet during the same speech, according to the Lusaka Times edition of June 07, 2012, His Excellency 'advised Zambians living abroad to return home and compete for jobs with their compatriots.' Clearly Mr. Sata appears to have forgotten why UK based Zambians had left their country in the first place.

Sata's opposition to dual citizenship was not born out of robust policy analysis or experience. It was probably no more than a knee jerk reaction that he thought would be popular especially among disadvantaged Zambians that formed the core of his constituency. This perhaps explains his statement during his London speech that he had a duty to protect the majority of Zambians 'especially poor citizens.'

The view that Sata's opposition to dual citizenship was not born out of analysis is fortified by an ambassadorial appointment made by the president early in his tenure. For his ambassador to Turkey, Sata chose a UK based nurse called Miriam Mwape Museba Mulenga Whittleton. Mrs. Whittleton was a British nurse of Zambian origin. In practical terms she enjoyed the benefits of citizenship in both the United Kingdom and the Republic of Zambia. This status was in violation of the Zambian Constitution at the time but that did not stop Mr. Sata from making the appointment. Perhaps the fact that Mrs. Whittleton was also his sister in law trumped constitutional niceties like the prohibition of dual citizenship.

Five months after the London meeting at which Sata warned of the dangers of dual citizenship, he appointed Professor Efford Clive Chirwa, as chief executive officer of the troubled national railway company, Zambia Railways Limited. Although born on the Zambian Copperbelt the new CEO spent most of his adult life in the United Kingdom and eventually became a British citizen.

A few years before retiring from his teaching position at Bolton University in the Greater Manchester Area, Chirwa started writing articles for a Zambian daily newspaper with a view to raising his profile in the country. His intention, declared from abroad, was to run for president. He must have known that his status as a British citizen would be problematic in this regard. And it is probably for this reason that he became an articulate advocate for dual citizenship. In one article he argued that but for colonialism he would have been entitled to three nationalities. He would have been Bemba by virtue of his mother's pre-colonial citizenship; Chewa by virtue of his father's origin, and Lamba by virtue of having been born in traditional Lamba territory.

Clearly Professor Chirwa took a dim view of Sata's opposition to dual citizenship and supported the approach of the Mung'omba Commission.

But while the Mung'omba approach represented an improvement on all previous constitutions save the 1964 one in this regard, it did raise concerns of its own. The Mung'omba recommendation effectively created two classes of citizens, contrary to the spirit and letter of the 1996 constitution which guaranteed equality of treatment for all citizens. Zambians by birth were accorded a superior status to Zambians by registration.

As some academics have pointed out, it should make no difference whether the Zambians by registration reside in Zambia or whether Zambians by birth reside abroad at the time their second citizenship is acquired. Susan Margaret Clayton fears, for example, that if implemented this provision could "breed resentment, discourage real integration and entrench anti-immigrant sentiments." These are not hollow fears. Most civil wars are a result of perceptions that one group is favoured over another. This kind of perceived discrimination was indeed the cause of the anti-colonial independence movement in Zambia.

It is time for Zambia to grasp the nettle and allow dual citizenship for all nationals regardless of ancestry. In addition to facilitating freer movement of Zambian skilled labour and better dissemination of information, dual nationality would have other more tangible economic benefits.

Opponents of dual citizenship cite security considerations and what they see as an absence of economic benefit to the country as reasons for not permitting non-indigenous Zambians from acquiring Zambian citizenship in addition to the citizenship of their countries of birth, as well as disallowing indigenous Zambians from acquiring foreign citizenships.

With respect to security considerations, the basic argument is that it is impossible to determine the loyalty of people with multiple citizenships. This is an argument that Mr. Sata himself employed in more lucid moments. At its most alarming level this argument goes on to suggest that dual citizenship increases the likelihood of espionage.

There is in fact no evidence for this proposition. The best known case of betrayal and disloyalty in the British Commonwealth is that of three Cambridge graduates who served in the British foreign office.

In 1951 two British diplomats, Guy Burgess and Donald MacLean, disappeared only to surface in Moscow five years later. The speculation was that the head of the Soviet section of the British Secret Intelligence Service had alerted Burgess and MacLean before they could be arrested for espionage. Indeed Harold "Kim" Philby had alerted Burgess and MacLean, as suspected. The three Cambridge graduates were the most successful spies recruited by the Soviet Union.

Burgess and Maclean as members of the British Foreign Office supplied secrets, including highly classified nuclear information as well as secrets relating to the formation of the North Atlantic Treaty Organisation (NATO). Philby joined MI-6 and eventually served as head of counterespionage operations after World War II and became the top British intelligence officer in Washington in 1949.

At the time of Burgess' and MacLean's disappearance in 1951, Allied counterintelligence had begun to suspect that Maclean was a Soviet mole. Philby got wind of this and told his friend Burgess to pass on the information to MacLean. Both Burgess and Maclean immediately fled to Moscow. Philby had saved his friends, but his close association with them soon directed attention to himself. He was relieved of his intelligence duties in 1951 and dismissed altogether from

MI-6 in 1956. By 1963 it was clear that counterintelligence was close to nabbing him, so he too fled to the Soviet Union.

Kim Philby died in Russia in 1988, and was buried with full honours in a Moscow cemetery. Burgess and MacLean also died there and buried in like fashion.

Burgess, Maclean, and Philby were British nationals with a traditional British education. Not one of them held another citizenship apart from their birth nationality. And yet they betrayed their country. They took their citizenship for granted, as indigenous people tend to.

In Zambia the best known espionage case is perhaps that of Webster Kayi Lumbwe. That case has been cited many times. Suffice it to say here that Lumbwe who was convicted of spying for America's Central Intelligence Agency was an indigenous Zambian who held no other citizenship.

The notion that there is an axiomatic link between dual citizenship and propensity toward espionage is plainly absurd. It is equally absurd to suggest in today's global economy that no economic benefits flow from dual citizenship.

Zambians in the Diaspora may not be looked upon favourably by some of their compatriots who accuse them of having 'abandoned' their homeland. In fact the Zambian Diaspora makes a quantifiable contribution to the national economy.

In October 2007, the International Fund for Agricultural Development, an arm of the United Nations and the Inter-American Development Bank, released the first complete map of worldwide remittances. The map compiled the best available information drawn from data collected on migrant populations, percentage of migrants sending remittances, average amounts remitted annually, as well as the average frequency of transfers. The map was exceptionally credible because it used central banks and other official government sources, money transfer companies, international organizations and academic institutions for reference support.

According to the map, Zambians in the Diaspora sent $201 million home in 2006. That represents 1.8 per cent of the country's gross domestic product at the time, and is more than the government received from mineral royalties.

The Diaspora does this under very difficult conditions. Zambia is one of the more expensive countries to send money to because of high bank charges. People now rarely send bank drafts to relations and friends at home because a $100 draft attracts a fee of $20. That is exorbitant. The result is that Zambians use money transfer companies and when it is not possible to do so they hang on to their money until they can find someone going home who would then physically deliver the cash. At the very least the high fees at home slow down the rate of remittances and sometimes encourage Zambian expatriates to abandon the idea altogether. But despite these difficulties the Diaspora continues to support the home economy. According to Daniel Mwamba the publisher of *UK Zambians,* the Zambian Diaspora remitted $300 million in 2010.

But the Diaspora can only do so much. The Zambian government needs to do its part too.

This is why in 2013 the Zambian Government was urged by the Lusaka based think tank, Policy Monitoring and Research Centre (PMRC), to put in place deliberate policies that would attract investment capital from Zambians living in the Diaspora.

According to PMRC, Zambians in the Diaspora were a 'national asset' that could contribute greatly to the country's economic development if appropriate policies were put in place.

PMRC specifically noted that Zambia could significantly benefit from the untapped economic potential of Zambians living in the Diaspora through remittances of money, capacity building, investment partnerships, skills and knowledge to boost economic development.

In order to achieve this, the think tank called for formulation of comprehensive Diaspora engagement policies aimed at removing barriers such as those arising from the ban on dual citizenship.

Lack of government support and extraordinarily high remittance fees explain, at least partly, the fall in Zambia's remittances in 2013. The remittances in that year amounted to $126 million. The figure represents official remittances and is probably an underestimate of the actual amount sent to Zambia from the Diaspora.

The reintroduction of dual citizenship by the Edgar Lungu government in early 2016 may well result in an increase in remittances into Zambia. Incidentally the new constitution avoids the problems of creating two classes of citizens as indicated above. The 2016 constitution simply states that 'a citizen shall not lose citizenship by acquiring the citizenship of another country.' Thus the stage is set for a potential increase in capital inflows as Zambians of all backgrounds abroad now have access to well-paying jobs reserved for citizens of the countries they have settled in.

There does appear to be a strong correlation between dual citizenship and remittance levels, as the Ghanaian and Indian experiences show.

In response to rising remittances from the Indian Diaspora at the turn of the century, the Indian government set out to effectively nullify the anti-dual nationality provisions in the law.

On December 22, 2003 the Indian Parliament passed a bill that effectively allowed dual citizenship for people of Indian origin. The bill which became law on 2nd December 2005 has helped grant dual citizenship to Persons of Indian Origin (PIOs) belonging to, or having citizenship of other countries subject to certain conditions. The grant of dual citizenship was intended to facilitate easier travel to and from India for Diaspora members who had taken foreign passports. It was also meant to encourage remittances from Indians abroad to their ancestral land.

The law appears to have worked. Whereas in 1996/1997 and 2003/2004 the Indian Reserve Bank reported remittances of $12.3 billion and $21 billion respectively, by 2008 these remittances had shot up to $45 billion. According to the Ministry of Overseas Indian Affairs, remittances to India stood at $67.6 billion in 2012-13, accounting for more than 4% of the country's gross domestic product. This then grew to $70 billion in 2013-14, the highest amongst the countries receiving remittances from overseas workers.

We can be sure that with the introduction of this law Indians who had previously emigrated but held back from acquiring a second passport for fear of losing their Indian nationality, were now able to do so and thus open for themselves new opportunities that increased their ability to earn more and send larger remittances home. For Indians who had taken out new citizenships and thus lost Indian citizenship, the original nationality was effectively restored and the possibility of returning to the homeland became a reality. For these Indians it made sense to send money back home and build a nest egg for retirement there.

The Ghanaian experience tells a similar story.

Ghana allowed dual citizenship in 2001. In 1990 Ghanaians living abroad sent $200 million home. A year after the new law came into force, remittances jumped to $680 million. In 2003 the Ghanaian Diaspora demonstrated its appreciation of dual citizenship by sending home a whopping $1 billion. Five years later that figure doubled. In 2012 the figure was a staggering $18.7 billion, according to the Bank of Ghana.

Clearly there are real economic benefits to be derived from dual citizenship.

Part Two
Anaemic Leadership

CHAPTER FIVE

A Foreman in Charge

Until he became President, Michael Sata had the reputation of a politician who got things done. He excelled as governor (mayor) of Lusaka by keeping the city relatively clean, building a new dual carriageway, and a flyover bridge that undoubtedly saved lives as pedestrians were no longer obliged to cross the main railway line as they moved from the eastern part of the city to the west and vice versa. He was always abrupt and reluctant to listen to alternative viewpoints. It was perhaps this trait that led Kenneth Kaunda to publicly observe that Sata simply did not have the temperament to be head of state. In 2006 Kaunda dismissed Sata as "not presidential material."

This viewpoint was quickly revised when Sata won the presidency in 2011 and Kaunda and his family became beneficiaries of that presidency.

But Kaunda's earlier opinion was not without merit. If a president is expected to listen respectfully to opposing views and to take those views into account when reaching decisions, then clearly Sata was not presidential material. If a president is expected to have a vision and the ability to articulate that vision consistently, again Mr. Sata would have fallen short.

Sata was never known for diplomacy or the ability to persuade through intellectual dialogue. His forte was taking action after the conceptualisation had been done and the plans drawn up. This may explain why his greatest success as head of state was expanding the country's physical infrastructure. Sata was at his best leading through action rather than through ideas. He was a conscientious foreman rather than a chief executive officer.

And this is the level at which he provided leadership.

There have of course been many apparently successful heads of state that did not possess classic chief executive skills and qualities. In these instances however the heads of state concerned understood their limitations and employed suitable advisers to address these shortcomings. And they listened to advice. Partly because of his poor health but mostly because of his temperament, Sata did not allow for the possibility that he may not have all the qualities necessary for effective presidential leadership, as his new ally Kaunda had once declared.

Sata's temperament and inability to understand the role of a chief executive officer led to authoritarian tendencies, erratic behaviour, and lack of direction. Indiscipline and even thuggery within his party resulted from Sata's failure to play the chief executive role effectively.

The saga of Statutory Instrument Number 89 (SI 89) is an example of Sata's authoritarian tendencies.

SI 89 was issued by the Finance Minister Alexander Bwalya Chikwanda. It ended the ten percent excise duty on the export of copper concentrate from Zambia. This tax had been imposed as a way of 'forcing' local mining companies to use local smelters. The tax was popular among politicians largely because they were uninformed about mining issues and failed to appreciate the negative economic impact the law would have.

Over time, it became clear that the tax was a threat to jobs and prosperity in Zambia. The myth that mining companies deliberately avoided using Zambian smelters was also exposed. The reason mining companies exported copper concentrate at great cost to them was that Zambia did not have enough smelting capacity in the country. When the tax on the export of copper concentrate was introduced, mining companies were therefore obliged to stockpile tons of the material until there was space in the local smelters. In the meantime, mines would place a moratorium on production of copper concentrate and in some instances laid off workers until the stocks had been exhausted and production was once again warranted. Delaying the treatment of copper concentrate also had the effect of delaying sales which in turn delayed corporate and other taxes payable to the exchequer. It was this latter effect of the tax on concentrate that motivated the Minister of Finance to act. The minister's actions were entirely rational and justified.

But on October 28, 2013 President Sata summoned the Zambia Revenue Authority Commissioner General Berlin Msiska to explain the non-collection of tax on copper concentrate exports.

Mr. Sata, without taking into account the explanations offered then directed that Statutory Instrument No 89 be revoked. His reason for revoking the statutory instrument was that it had the effect of depriving Zambians of jobs. How this happened was never explained. The President was quoted as follows by *the Post* newspaper:

> Honourable Finance Minister, Zambians you are depriving them of jobs by...you want me to exempt duty on this soil by ZCCM or KCM you want to export to South Africa. Now, if today Honourable Minister of Finance you start exporting Zambian soil and you exempt them from paying duty, where is the customs general?

The President did not limit his criticism to the Minister of Finance. He was equally unhappy with the Commissioner General whom he addressed as follows:

> They are not going to pay tax, excise duty and you tell your minister 'sign statutory instrument to export soil', and you don't know what is contained in that soil? The minister cannot sign without you advising him. What is the explanation...When they

process those materials, were they going to come back to Zambia…At 40 years old, you are supposed to be more reasonable than me. You export to South Africa and they will not come back to Zambia and you advise the minister, 'sign no excise duty'. What should I do to you? Mr. ZRA Commissioner General Berlin Msiska, where are you? Is there any logic for us to advise the Honourable Minister to export soil? They can go and dig the whole tipper truck and export to South Africa and you have the so-called commissioner of tax. You two must have recommended to the minister. Where? Forty nine years of independence, you are exporting soil! Even the forefathers who died on the mines in 1943 mines strikes, you would have not been where you are today. You don't want all that. Anyway, the two of you get out of this meeting, go and prepare the revocation for this Statutory Instrument.

The incoherence on the part of the head of state was neither unusual nor solely a result of anger. Much of Sata's presidency was characterised by the issuance of statements that were disjointed and often irrelevant to the occasion. This led to concerns about the President's health. But these concerns were quickly dismissed by the state machinery controlled by persons with a vested interest in the continuance of the Sata presidency.

On one occasion as Zambia's 50th independence anniversary was approaching, President Sata invited prominent senior citizens for lunch at State House. He understandably paid tribute to his wife Christine Kaseba. The message however had something of a higgledy-piggledy flavour. Consider the following:

This girl you have seen here without her probably by now I would have been rotten. I would have died a long time ago. And this young man (Grey Zulu) you have seen here was my boss, he was secretary general of the United National Independence Party (UNIP); without him there would be no Zambia. His brother

(Dr. Kenneth Kaunda) is not here. Is the secretary general of the party here? Mr. Wynter! Secretary General has not been feeling well… We are the only country with a female Chief Justice, that's why there's a lot of justice in the judiciary.

It was not unreasonable to ask whether the president was on anabolic steroids which can trigger aggressive behaviour. If the president was on steroids, what was he being treated for? The president and his team reacted to the question by insisting the leader was well.

These assurances did nothing to quell speculation that Michael Sata was gravely ill. The frequent foreign visits for medical treatment only added to the nation's anxiety.

One foreign trip that caused particular anxiety was the visit to Israel in July 2014. The trip was hastily organised and unlike other trips was shrouded in secrecy, with the head of state leaving the country and returning under cover of darkness. For three weeks prior to the trip, the president had not been seen in public. He had not even made postings on Facebook, his favourite way of communicating with the nation.

Disingenuously, the president's handlers sought to hide Sata's frailty by only publishing pictures taken at a distance. The Zambian population quickly saw through this and became even more convinced that their president was unwell.

In his first post on Facebook after the three week hiatus, Sata was reasonably coherent. Of course the posting was drafted by an official in the government. It focused on infrastructure development, the area Sata was most comfortable with. Here is an excerpt:

Today, I wish to share with you our Government's efforts to connect rural communities which include schools, rural health centres, chiefs' palaces, local courts, staff houses for Government employees and other Government facilities to the Power Grid. Our Government through the Rural Electrification Authority

(REA) intends to commission some of the grid extension projects that have been implemented from 2012 to date in Southern, Copperbelt, North-Western, Western and Eastern Provinces as follows:

1. Mwanza Kasaka Grid Extension Project, Monze District, Southern Province: this project involved the construction of a total 67.7km of 11kV overhead line from an existing line at Kaumba Basic School in Monze district at a cost of K15,235,000;

2. Mbeza Grid Extension Project, Namwala District, Southern Province: this project involves the construction of a total of 44.4km of 33kV of overhead grid lines from an existing 33kV line from Choma to Namwala District passing through Niko Rural Growth Centre at a cost of K11,172,000;

The handling of the president's health was one of the starkest examples of inadequate leadership during the Sata years. Every move made by the government provoked a negative reaction and raised more questions. The diatribe and anxiety could have been avoided simply by admitting that the president was unwell and making arrangements for the president to seek appropriate treatment and recuperate. Matters were of course made worse by the fact that Sata had done nothing to clarify whether or not Vice President Guy Scott could constitutionally act as interim president. As indicated earlier, Sata could have sought a court order to clarify the matter.

In the absence of this leadership, other political players and civil society started to weigh in with suggestions. Thus the civil rights activist, Brebner Changala petitioned the High Court to compel the government to constitute a medical board with the mandate of examining the physical and mental health of President Michael Sata. The matter was allocated to Mr. Justice Isaac Chali of the High Court sitting at Ndola.

Changala, a paralegal by training, was not unfamiliar with legal proceedings. He stated in his application that he had been forced to seek judicial review following the president's obvious frailty when he appeared in public as well as the president's incoherent public speeches that had fuelled speculation about his health. Changala observed that there had been an obvious decline in Mr. Sata's health since he assumed office. He referred to the president's visit to Israel and the unusual circumstances of that visit as evidence that the president was not well.

The principle justification for Changala's action was that it had become absolutely necessary in the public interest to consider the question of the physical and mental capacity of the president so as to ascertain the head of state's physical and mental wellbeing. Changala conceded that ordinarily this task would be left to the cabinet but then argued that cabinet had failed to perform its duty as outlined in the Constitution.

Mr. Justice Chali was unimpressed with Mr. Changala's arguments. He refused to grant leave for judicial review, finding that the application lacked merit and was actually frivolous and vexatious. Mr. Justice Chali further found that Mr. Changala had failed to show sufficient interest in the matter as a private citizen.

The judge went on to discredit the evidence provided by Mr. Changala, saying there was no evidence that the cabinet had failed to table the motion on the President's health.

It was within the judge's discretion to accept or reject the evidence furnished by Mr. Changala. It was not however reasonable for the judge to find that Mr. Changala, as a private citizen, had no interest in the health of President Sata. Every citizen is interested in the health of his or her president. In democracies state presidents work for people like Mr.

Changala who put them in office. The health of these presidents would be something of concern to them.

The judiciary's refusal to intervene and pave the way for a formal declaration of the president's incapacity only intensified calls for action in the political arena. A novel approach in this regard came from the level headed leader of the National Restoration Party (NAREP) Mr. Elias Chipimo Jr.

On May 11, 2014 the NAREP leader called on opposition parties to rally behind a non-partisan presidential candidate in the 2016 general election. This candidate would, in the event of election, serve for a period of nine months. In effect the candidate would serve as interim president with the primary responsibility of facilitating the enactment of a new constitution.

Even as he planned for the 2016 election, Mr. Chipimo predicted that Zambia would be thrown into early elections because of the President's poor health.

In suggesting an interim presidency led by a non-partisan player committed to the introduction of a new constitution, Chipimo was responding to past experience and the failure of successive governments to implement constitutional provisions popular with the Zambian population. It was important to have an interim president whose time and mandate in office would be limited. Chipimo believed that normally politicians ascending to the presidency shun any reform that take away political power because of re-election concerns and a deep desire to stay in power. In this regard, he cited President Frederick Chiluba's disingenuous attempt to run for a constitutionally unauthorised third term as an example. The solution therefore, according to the NAREP leader, was to have a president with no vested interest in maintaining the constitutional status quo.

The question raised by commentators and indeed fellow opposition leaders was, 'How do we ensure that the interim president will step down after the nine months and actually implement the constitutional reforms he or she was elected to effect?' Chipimo, always the consummate lawyer, found his answer in legal procedure. The non-partisan presidential candidate would be required to sign an undated letter of resignation as a condition of nomination by the Opposition. Furthermore the undated letter of resignation would be registered with the High Court for Zambia.

Whether or not Mr. Chipimo's proposal would have worked is less important than the fact that Mr. Chipimo and (by extension) the Opposition were at least taking leadership and considering options. No such leadership came from the government despite the fact that by August 2014 President Sata had not been seen in public for several weeks.

Even with mounting evidence that the President was not well, the government continued to maintain that the 77-year-old head of state was in good health and continuing to discharge his duties normally. Any chief executive officer would have vetoed the propagation of this viewpoint as normal functions for a head of state include being seen in public.

This public bravado however could not mask the truth within the government and the PF. Inevitably, the president's poor health and the failure of the government to admit that the head of state was unwell, led to subterranean but real jockeying for power.

The failure of adequate leadership in managing the president's health issue, led to uninformed speculation and crude analysis that in some cases could not have been further from the truth.

There was talk of two main factions emerging. One of these factions was said to be mainly Bemba speaking, led by the cosmopolitan Finance Minister Alexander Chikwanda. His major accomplices in this regard were said to be former Defence Minister Godfrey Bwalya Mwamba and President Sata's son, Mulenga who served as mayor of Lusaka. The second group was said to be led by Vice President Guy Scott, Justice Minister and PF Secretary-General Wynter Kabimba, former Tourism Minister Sylvia Masebo. Kabimba was seen by these analysts as Sata's preferred successor.

How wrong 'analysts' can be!

Sata did of course die, but not before he had fired Wynter Kabimba as Minister of Justice and Secretary-General of the PF. Despite the fact that on his last trip abroad Sata had asked Edgar Lungu, the new Minister of Justice who also served as Minister of Defence and secretary general of the party, to act as President, Lungu immediately handed power over to Guy Scott when the president's death was announced.

Mulenga Sata declared his intention to seek the PF nomination so that he could run for president in the special election but on further reflection changed his mind. Godfrey Bwalya Mwamba also declared his intention to run. He was not successful and when Edgar Lungu emerged as party president, Mwamba decided to back him, only to change his mind later and 'endorse' a candidate from a different party altogether. Alexander Bwalya Chikwanda maintained a low profile, but gave critical support to Edgar Lungu's campaign. In May 2016 Guy Scott and Mulenga Sata, alleged by the 'analysts' to be in opposing camps, both left the PF to support Mr. Hichilema's UPND opposition party.

The factions had not been as clear cut as the 'analysts' had assessed.

In fairness to these analysts however, they were bound to get it wrong given how poorly the information about the president's health was managed and how little credible information was allowed to enter the public domain.

CHAPTER SIX

Bad Decisions

The decision to conceal the President's health and thereby unleash the creative rumour mill is not the only overtly bad decision made during the Sata presidency. Because of President Sata's impatience with elaborate advice and advisers, a number of unforced errors characterised the populist's tenure in office. These errors were both substantive and procedural.

One of the most puzzling errors occurred within a week of Michael Sata assuming the presidency.

As already pointed out, the constitution allows the president after a general election to the National Assembly and before the National Assembly is next dissolved, to appoint such number of persons as he considers necessary to enhance representation in the National Assembly with respect to interests or skills. The Constitution is also explicit that there cannot be more than eight such members at any one time.

This provision was debated intensely in 1991 as Zambia was re-establishing democracy. Mr. Sata was involved in these discussions. And yet on September 29, 2011 Sata appointed Bob Sichinga, Ngosa Simbyakula, John Phiri, Panji Kaunda, Samuel Mukupa, Sebastian Zulu, Willie Nsanda, Alexander Chikwanda, Solomon Mbuzi and Joseph Kasonde to parliament. The nominees were also appointed as cabinet and deputy ministers. But there was a problem; the president had nominated two parliamentarians too many.

Surely from his participation in the constitutional discussions he should have known that he had exceeded his powers. It is of course possible that he had forgotten the issue after such a long time. In that case should his instinct not have been to consult the Attorney-General who is the government's principal legal advisor? Indeed he could have consulted his newly minted friend Kenneth Kaunda who had made many such appointments over his 27 years as president of the Republic.

The answer perhaps lies in the fact that Sata was an action leader rather than a thought leader. Seeking advice with a view to establishing the theoretical framework for decisions was not part of his instinctual makeup. This aspect of Sata's character came to the fore time and time again and led to bad decisions. The Chitimukulu saga is a case in point.

The Chitimukulu is the paramount monarch of the Bemba, the largest collection of ethnic groups in Zambia. The chieftainship is named after Chiti Mukulu (Chiti the Great), who in the 18th century carved out the Bemba nation from the Lunda Empire of Mwata Yamvu.

About six months before Sata's ascendency to the presidency, the head of the Bemba chieftaincy, Chitimukulu Chilufya Mwango Chitapankwa III died. In April 2012, Henry Kanyanta Sosala, the then Chief Mwamba, assumed the position of Chitimukulu in accordance with Bemba law and tradition. But despite being formally recognised by *Ba Shilubemba*, the only body empowered to recognise the Chitimukulu, President Sata declined to issue a formal Notice of Recognition in the *Government Gazette*.

No credible reason for withholding formal recognition was articulated by the Head of State or indeed anyone else in the government. But the reasons given by the active Zambian rumour mill ranged from a conspiracy by Sata's clan within the Bemba group to dominate other Bembas to a vendetta by Sata for humiliation he suffered several years earlier at the hands of Sosala in his private capacity.

Why would Sata for apparently flimsy reasons risk alienating an important constituency of the country? Indeed given the history of the Bemba and their relationships with other groups, Sata was jeopardising his own party's success in the entire country at the next general election. And yet Sata appeared in no hurry to settle the matter. On the contrary he ordered his Minister for Chiefs and Traditional Affairs, Nkandu Luo, to defend the indefensible.

The Honourable Minister of Chiefs and Traditional Affairs did not disappoint her leader. She called for the arrest of Kanyanta Sosala for acting illegally as a traditional ruler. In so doing she predictably provoked the ire of the opposition parties and even members of her own PF party.

One of the more coherent criticisms of the minister came from General Godfrey Miyanda, head of the Heritage Party. He called for the minister to be recusant in matters pertaining to the Bemba Royal Establishment because it had become clear that she was using her position to wage a personal vendetta against Mr. Sosala. The reference to the personal vendetta again reinforced the idea in the court of public opinion that the government was withdrawing formal recognition of the paramount chief for purely personal reasons. While recognising the personal nature of the disagreement between the Paramount Chief and the Minister (and by extension the President) Miyanda noted that this dispute was contributing to division in the nation.

The best evidence we have that the failure to formally recognise Paramount Chief Chitimukulu was frivolous and unrelated to state wellbeing perhaps lies in the fact that within days of being sworn in as the new president, Edgar Chagwa Lungu, issued the formal recognition.

Paramount Chief Chitimukulu

CHAPTER SEVEN

Invisible Leadership

While few would agree that Michael Chilufya Sata was ever a thought leader, the consensus would surely be that in the years preceding his presidency, he was an obvious action leader. He was after all the man who (as mayor) expanded Lusaka's infrastructure at a time of severe financial constraint. He kept his city clean and when he left office, the city's finances were in the healthiest state they had been for a long time. This was a result of Sata providing disciplined leadership to the Council and establishing a number of revenue generating ventures that helped the Council to eliminate its historic deficit.

Downtown Lusaka

As Minister of health, Sata regularly toured hospitals and often fired underperforming nurses on the spot. His visible leadership led to a marked improvement in the delivery of health services.

As president however Sata often withheld visible leadership when it was most needed. This appears to have been a result of illness rather than choice. Whatever the reason, the absence of leadership had negative consequences. Some of the consequences were an increase in violence, disregard of the law, and even missed economic opportunities.

On Saturday April 14, 2014 the UPND leader Hakainde Hichilema narrowly escaped lynching from armed PF cadres who were opposed to Mr. Hichilema being interviewed by an Ndola radio station.

The PF thugs dressed in blue aprons and armed with pistols, machetes, and other objects, blocked the entrance of the commercial building where the radio station was housed, with the stated intention of assaulting Mr. Hichilema.

Realising that the PF cadres, reinforced by other political thugs from the neighbouring town of Kitwe, were intent on violently disrupting Hichilema's programme and even destroying the station's building, the radio station's staff called the police.

The cadres were clearly indifferent to Hichilema's constitutional right to seek support for his political platform. They did not believe Hichilema had a right to campaign in 'their' territory. One of them was quoted by the *Post* newspaper on April 14 as saying:

All we want is HH. We have told UPND that Copperbelt is a no go area for him [Hichilema]. We want to burn him alive with a tyre.

The violence perpetrated by the political hooligans was serious, resulting in injury to UPND supporters and damage to a car parked near the station. Mr. Hichilema himself was able to escape, shaken, but physically unharmed.

This behaviour should be condemned by everyone, but especially by democratically elected leaders. Violence and democracy are incompatible. Sadly, there was no response from the head of state about the violence. The only voice from the ruling party to offer anything resembling condemnation of the savagery came from Mr. Wynter Kabimba the party secretary general. His condemnation was however far from categorical. Mr. Kabimba qualified his response by saying "if indeed those who wanted to attack Hichilema were members of the PF" they should heed his message about discipline within and outside the party.

Mr. Kabimba must have been the only person aware of the incident who did not know who the perpetrators were. Kabimba did nevertheless add usefully that PF members should accept that Zambia was a democracy and competitive politics required tolerance.

Unfortunately he went on to undermine himself by adding:

> But I also want to say this that we also as Patriotic Front get very disappointed when members of the opposition political parties do not concentrate on the programmes that they intend to undertake if ever they came to power, or in the unlikely event that they came to power. You do not hear this from the UPND or the MMD. Instead what you hear are just inflammatory statements, insults against President Michael Sata and insults against the leadership of the Patriotic Front. So I think this thing is a scale on both sides.

This was no time to blame the victim. What was required was an affirmation of constitutional rights like freedom of assembly and freedom of speech. Mr. Hichilema was in Ndola precisely to explain to the people of the Copperbelt Province what programs his party would institute in the event of coming to power. The appropriate response for the ruling party when they disagreed with the UPND was to state their own position in an appropriate forum, not to threaten violence against legitimate political opponents.

But these threats took place because restless young members of the PF saw an absence of leadership committed to managing democratic order. And they were justified in assuming there was a leadership vacuum. After all, the leader of the party remained silent throughout the ordeal and the Secretary-General's condemnation of the egregious behaviour witnessed in Ndola was qualified and lukewarm.

Indeed the PF cadres saw a leader who himself was willing to publicly disregard the law when this suited him. In instances where the president breached the law he could very easily have sought advice from his attorney general or other colleagues with the necessary experience. Why did he not do this?

The answer lay at least in part in President Sata's impatient character. Sata was a man of action with little time for what he considered niceties and mere details. He was not one to spend too much time conceptualising and investing in theoretical analysis. Because of this some economic opportunities for Zambia were lost during Sata's presidency.

For example, the debate about the global shift toward cleaner growth had already started when Mr. Sata became president. One of his opponents, Elias Chipimo, understood the importance of clean growth and made green energy a cornerstone of his platform. Sata never truly appreciated the significance of this. Even his populist instincts would not lead him to understand that shifting toward cleaner growth would, if done properly, lead to thousands possibly tens of thousands of new jobs. There were studies the president could have relied on to get a better understanding of how clean technology could help Zambia.

It is of course unreasonable to expect a president to read every single study on every subject, but that is not what was expected of President Sata. He could have discharged his duty by simply having respectful conversations with his economic and social policy advisors. Surely the president would have understood from these conversations that the world was running into the earth's ecological limits, resulting in growing levels of scarcity of many natural resources.

These two drivers alone pose an environmental challenge but also offer a huge economic opportunity. Countries and companies that respond appropriately to the challenge could reap huge benefits.

But in a country like Zambia these benefits cannot be realised without the government playing a key role, targeting investment, maximising performance of workers, building infrastructure including smart grid and offering real incentives for investment. President Sata could have used his unique ability to communicate with ordinary Zambians to create a new culture of entrepreneurship.

Less than four years after the start of the Sata presidency, the importance of clean energy and the critical role African economies could play were placed at the centre of the economic development conversation as a result of President Barack Obama's visit to Kenya and Ethiopia.

On July 25, 2015, President Barack Obama observed that African countries had the opportunity to avoid dependency on fossil fuel and other forms of dirty energy, and move straight to clean and renewable energy. The President, who spoke during a visit to the Power Africa Innovation Fair in Nairobi, noted further that the growing use of environment friendly energy sources, such as solar power, to generate electricity promised a bright future for the continent.

On the same day that President Obama delivered this optimistic message in Kenya, electricity supply to Zambia's largest copper mine and the biggest contributor to the Zambian exchequer, Kansanshi Mining Plc, was reduced from the steady-state level of 153 megawatts to 117 megawatts. Electricity supply at the Kansanshi related Greenfield Sentinel Project, was also reduced to 42 megawatts from 55 megawatts.

Elsewhere in the country some households were kept in darkness for as much as ten hours a day because of load shedding. It is a matter of deep regret that Sata and his predecessors never took the interest in clean energy that Mr. Chipimo and his small party have taken.

In fairness to Sata however he was more willing to expand and rehabilitate infrastructure than most of his predecessors.

The early years of Zambia's statehood were characterised by growth in infrastructure as the new government sought to redress historical imbalances in development between black and white Zambia. The government embarked on an infrastructure-development programme that included new roads, new schools, new hospitals, and even a microwave link that allowed all Zambians (not just those on the Copperbelt Province) to watch television.

The post-independence government was not however always prudent in the use of resources. This, in addition to the drop in copper earnings, greatly affected infrastructure development which had almost come to a complete stop by the end of the 1970s.

The matter was not given real attention again until Frederick Chiluba took over the presidency and privatised key parts of the economy. But Chiluba's own plan to expand infrastructure was undermined by International Monetary Fund (IMF) limits on the country's borrowing. Had Chiluba been more imaginative and perhaps less obsequious to the IMF he would have made a case for infrastructure development, IMF limits on borrowing notwithstanding.

But there was private sector driven infrastructure development during the Chiluba and Mwanawasa years. After President Mwanawasa's death, the government of Rupiah Banda showed enthusiasm for infrastructure development by building an impressive network of new schools. But Banda too was constrained by money.

His successor, Michael Sata found a way. Within two years of taking office, the PF government went to the international debt market twice to raise money for infrastructure development. The first such initiative was a 10-year bond issued on September 13, 2012 and priced at 5.625%. The government had originally planned to raise $500 million but high levels of interest led it to increase the target to $750 million. Barclays and Deutsche Bank, the joint lead managers and book runners, said at the time that they had received more than 425 orders worth $12 billion.

In April 2014 Zambia sold $1 billion in what turned out to be Africa's first sovereign dollar-debt offer of the year at an interest rate more than 300 basis points higher than its 2012 debut issue. The significantly higher interest rate of 8.5 per cent reflected concern over the widening fiscal deficit that had prompted a ratings downgrade in 2013. Even so, the offer was about four times oversubscribed. The proceeds of this bond were earmarked for energy and transportation infrastructure.

The two Eurobonds enabled the populist Mr. Sata to draw up (and in some cases simply revisit) ambitious infrastructure plans, particularly for roads. In public statements Sata often complained about the potholes that blighted many of the country's roads. He intended to do something about this.

If Sata calculated that expanding infrastructure would help him and his party politically, he was right. There were expressions of open gratitude in places like Luapula province, where Mr. Sata's governing party, the Patriotic Front (PF), did well in the 2011 elections. But there was also praise from other provinces where the president's party had not done particularly well in the elections. The Western Province is a case in point.

Bright Tombi the mayor of Mongu, the provincial capital, was in no doubt that "Michael Sata's development agenda in the Western Province was unstoppable." Mr. Tombi was quoted by *the Post* as follows:

> In Mongu district, I am telling you that where infrastructure development is concerned, I think the PF has done its best. MMD had been in power for 20 years, it has just been making promissory notes. When it comes to infrastructure development, I think we are the best. I want to support the words of the Member of Parliament for Kalabo, Chinga Miyutu when he says that praise someone when they are still alive and not when they are dead…We have done the best and there is no doubt that everyone who lives in the Western Province is admiring what the PF is doing. Whatever the government intends to do in Western Province, no one will take it away from them. So in Mongu I will make sure that we shall keep working and encouraging His Excellency and other relevant bodies who want to bring development here so that Mongu changes.

Mr. Sata's critics charged however that the improvements were concentrated in PF strongholds and that infrastructure development was motivated only by political considerations. There was never any evidence for the claim that Mr. Sata concentrated infrastructure development in his strongholds.

Throughout Mr. Sata's presidency, the PF party had only one parliamentary seat in the Southern Province (worse representation than in the Western Province where they had two.) And yet, the Sata government invested in construction of roads and bridges with a view to linking up all towns in the South. Developing the Southern Province was in fact critical to Sata's strategy of boosting tourism and increasing trade with neighbouring countries like Zimbabwe, Zambia's southern neighbour.

This kind of commitment to the development of Zambia's infrastructure makes it all the more regrettable that by the time Sata got into office he was so seriously ill as to be incapable of effective visible leadership on a consistent basis. This form of leadership includes three key components: setting a vision, actively discussing the change, and knowing the impact.

During the campaign preceding the election, Sata executed the first responsibility for a leader who wants to visibly and proactively drive change, splendidly. He created a crystal clear vision of what the future would look like for the many low income Zambians that supported him. Studies of the electronic records of his rallies show that Sata communicated his vision with passion. It is for this reason that so many people believed that Sata would indeed be able to deliver a new constitution, new houses, and an entirely new social order within 90 days of assuming office.

But if Sata delivered the first requirement of visible leadership well, he was less successful with respect to the second and third requirements which focus on active discussion of the change and knowledge of the impact of the change.

Change leaders leave nothing to chance. They are out and about talking about the proposed change and winning converts until the change happens. With his illness, Sata could not do this.

Again for health reasons Mr. Sata was not able to know the impact of change in the country. The president was unable to focus on the task of identifying threats and obstacles to the desired change and addressing these threats and obstacles in a methodical manner. For example, Sata was always clear that Zambia should do more to protect its sovereignty and project an image to foreigners consistent with the country's sovereignty. He certainly told me this and often warned about the dangers of neo colonialism. He was also keen to invest in infrastructure believing that previous regimes had neglected infrastructure development because they lacked the will, imagination, and discipline to attend to this pressing issue. The third major change he wanted was gender equality and more opportunities for women.

Because of his illness Sata was not able to be out and about talking about the proposed change and winning converts with a view to effecting the necessary change. Instead the good message was clouded by concern and speculation about the president's health. Sata's own colleagues did not help. They feared that the leader was too ill to continue. In the circumstances implementation of Sata's vision was subordinated to other 'priorities' as his close colleagues manoeuvred to influence the choice of his successor, should Sata cease suddenly to be president.

The infighting became so intense that far from implementing change, President Sata found himself serving as custodian of the status quo. The corporate leadership found itself incapable of making difficult decisions. The government's fact finding mission was undermined and calculated risks (essential to good leadership) could not be taken. Obsession with winning the undeclared succession battle denied the combatants the ability to see the unique opportunities presented by Sata's initial vision.

Reducing Sata to a status quo president, together with the lack of cohesion and clarity at the highest levels of Zambian government inevitably resulted in mistakes that could have been easily avoided.

CHAPTER EIGHT

Unforced Errors

The absence of firm executive leadership, whether brought on by illness or temperament led to contradictions and absurdities both within the PF party and within the government. Not infrequently the nation was left wondering whether anyone was in charge at all. Sometimes protagonists with opposing viewpoints would quote the same presidential authority for their positions.

One example is the expulsion of Benjamin Siwila as Lusaka District PF vice secretary. The expulsion was reported in the *Zambia Daily Nation* on 10 June 2014. It is clear from the article than even this reputable newspaper was struggling to grasp the basic facts.

The confusion started when the expelled politician while acknowledging receipt of the expulsion letter, denied that he had actually been expelled. The basis of his dispute was that the letter purporting to expel him had not been authored by the president. Instead the letter was written by the party secretary general, Mr. Wynter Kabimba. For this reason Mr. Siwila decided to ignore the expulsion letter.

The article referred to above is not clear on the issue but it appears from surrounding circumstances that Mr. Siwila believed that Kabimba had misread the president's mind and based his letter on the *assumption* that the party leader wanted Siwila expelled. According to Siwila, the president's target was not him but a Julius Komaki, the PF Lusaka Town Centre Branch Chairman.

Siwila considered himself to be on firm ground in this belief. He had apparently attended a meeting at which

President Sata had ordered the expulsion of Mr. Komaki. But according to Mr. Siwila this order did not extend to him.

The reason Kabimba was keen to take this action, according to Siwila, was rooted in his 'hatred towards party cadres' who were demanding his dismissal and expulsion from the party. The purported expulsion came at a time when Mr. Kabimba was seen as Sata's chosen successor. The expulsions would be seen by many both within and without the ruling party as a purge of partisans likely to oppose Mr. Kabimba's ascension to the presidency.

We have already seen how politically damaging and anxiety inducing the unnecessary decision to withhold recognition of Henry Kanyanta Sosala as Chitimukulu was. We can also be certain that decisions like this were not without consequence.

On July 16, 2014, Patrick Mucheleka an independent Member of Parliament rose to ask the government how many police officers had been deployed at Paramount Chief Chitimukulu's palace between October 2013 and January 2014 in an effort to prevent the duly selected Chitimukulu from occupying his official residence. The MP also wanted to know how much the exercise had cost.

The Government's answer was delivered by the Home Affairs Deputy Minister Steven Kampyongo who told the House that a total of K499, 207.81 (US$ 79,239.33) had been spent on the operations. The bulk of that money (US$ 37,436.82) had been spent on allowances for police officers.

Although this amount may not be huge by the standards of high income countries, it is a colossal sum in a low middle income country like Zambia where (according to the World Bank) 60.5 per cent of the population lives in abject poverty. Patrick Mucheleka, who also served as Executive Director of Civic Society for Poverty Reduction, would have been acutely aware of this. In this vein the Member of Parliament asked a supplementary question aimed at ascertaining the nature of the threat that made it necessary for the government to deploy such a large number of police officers in the area. According to the *Lusaka Times* edition of July 16, 2014, the otherwise extremely able Minister of Home Affairs, Ngosa Simbyakula, could only observe that "the police found it necessary to enhance security in view of the uncertainty that was perceived to occur in the area."

This must have been an embarrassing moment for the Honourable Minister. The uncertainty he complained of had been caused by his boss!

Yet another unforced error that could have been avoided if only President Sata had made himself receptive to legal advice, was the appointment of Ms. Lombe Chibesakunda as acting Chief Justice of Zambia.

In June 2012 Chief Justice Ernest Sakala was pressured into prematurely terminating his contract of service. He was replaced by Madam Justice Lombe Chibesakunda. Under the Zambian Constitution, the president's appointment of a substantive chief justice must be confirmed by Parliament. The relevant provision of the constitution is article 93 which is reproduced below:

(1) The Chief Justice and Deputy Chief Justice shall, subject to ratification by the National Assembly, be appointed by the President.
(2) The judges of the Supreme Court shall, subject to ratification by the National Assembly, be appointed by the President.
(3) If the office of Chief Justice is vacant or if the Chief Justice is on leave or is for any reason
unable to perform the functions of that office, then, until a person has been appointed to, and has
assumed the functions of, that office or until the person holding that office has resumed those functions, as the case may be, the President may appoint the Deputy Chief Justice or a Supreme Court judge to perform such functions.

(4) Without prejudice to the generality of clause (5), if the office of Deputy Chief Justice is vacant or the Deputy Chief Justice is on leave or is for any other reason unable to perform the functions of his office, the President may appoint another judge of the Supreme Court to act as Deputy Chief Justice.

(5) If the office of a Supreme Court judge is vacant, or if any Supreme Court judge is appointed to act as Chief Justice or Deputy Chief Justice, or if any Supreme Court judge is on leave or is for any reason unable to perform the functions of that office, the President may appoint a person qualified for appointment as a judge of the Supreme Court to act as a Supreme Court judge.

(6) A person may act as the Chief Justice, Deputy Chief Justice or a Supreme Court judge notwithstanding that he has attained the age prescribed by Article 98.

(6) A puisne judge appointed to act as Deputy Chief Justice or Supreme Court judge, as the case may be, pursuant to clause (4) or (5), shall continue to be a judge of the High Court and may continue to perform the functions of the office of puisne judge.

As will be seen from the article, the republican president appoints the Deputy Chief Justice to act as chief justice in the event of a vacancy in the latter office. But Mr. Sata had also encouraged the premature termination of tenure of the acting Deputy Chief Justice, Dennis Chirwa. The substantive Deputy Chief Justice, Irene Mambilima, had earlier been seconded to the Electoral Commission of Zambia. In the circumstances, President Sata was justified in seeking a replacement chief justice from the ranks of the Supreme Court.

President Sata chose Madam Justice Lombe Chibesakunda, Zambia's first female lawyer. Mrs. Justice Chibesakunda has an impressive résumé. She was called to the Bar at Gray's Inn in 1969. She then served as state advocate for six years before trying her hand at private practice for a year. She went back to the public sector in 1973 to serve as Solicitor General, Deputy Minister of Legal Affairs, and Member of Parliament for the Lusaka constituency of Matero. In addition to these accomplishments she also served as ambassador to Japan and high commissioner to the United Kingdom.

Her foray into the judiciary started with an appointment as chair of the industrial relations court. She ended up as a Supreme Court judge. It was from these ranks that Michael Chilufya Sata selected her for the chief justice position.

From the outset the appointment attracted controversy. A number of lawyers observed that the new chief justice designate was 68, three years older than the usual retirement age for a chief justice. Reference was made to the fact that Mr. Justice Sakala had stepped down at least in part because he was over the age of 65. (It should also be noted that a president may permit a judge who has attained the age of 65 to continue in office for such period as may be necessary to enable her to deliver judgement or to do any other thing in relation to proceedings that were commenced before her before she attained the age of 65. The President may also appoint a judge of the High Court in accordance with the advice of the Judicial Service Commission or a judge of the Supreme Court, who has attained the age of sixty-five years, for such further period, not exceeding seven years, as he may determine.)

When President Sata submitted Chibesakunda's name for ratification to the parliamentary select committee, her age became an issue and the committee rejected the nominee. Despite this rejection, President Sata insisted that Madam Justice Chibesakunda continue to act as chief justice. And she did.

Predictably the rumour mill went into overtime with theories as to why Sata was insisting on Chibesakunda's appointment. The fact that the president and the acting chief justice both hailed from the same clan within the Bemba ethnic group, did not help matters. It was suggested that this bond would allow Sata to influence the judiciary in politically charged legal cases to the electoral advantage of the ruling party. The then leader of the opposition, Nevers Mumba, reportedly accused the president of seeking to influence the outcome of parliamentary election petition appeals before the Supreme Court. These appeals had been brought by unsuccessful Patriotic Front parliamentary candidates.

The atmosphere was so poisoned it was safe to say Madam Justice Lombe Chibesakunda was never going to be accepted in her Chief Justice role by the legal fraternity. Indeed some of her own fellow judges privately found the acting Chief Justice's position unattainable. At this point Chibesakunda and the president should have made an exit plan that would have had the acting Chief Justice leaving voluntarily and on her terms. They did not, and the controversy continued.

In September 2013 the Law Association of Zambia took the unusual step of petitioning the High Court for Zambia with a view to ending Madam Justice Chibesakunda's tenure as acting Chief Justice. The petition argued that since the acting Chief Justice had reached the retirement age for a Supreme Court Judge at the time of her appointment, the President could not appoint her to the position of chief justice although he could have extended her contract as a Supreme Court judge.

The second ground in the petition was that in any event President Sata could not renew Madam Justice Chibesakunda's contract because under the law a judge's contract could only be renewed once. This argument was made in light of the fact that former President Rupiah Banda had renewed Chibesakunda's contract in 2009 for a period of three years.

The Law Association of Zambia gave the acting Chief Justice a one month ultimatum to vacate the office. The ultimatum was of course ignored by Sata whose response was to insinuate that the petition itself may have been criminally motivated. While swearing in members of a tribunal (set up in doubtful circumstances) to probe the conduct of two high court judges, the president claimed that "criminals in the judiciary" were undermining the acting Chief Justice.

In the end however the Law Association of Zambia got it's way, albeit in an unexpected manner. Within a few days of being sworn in as new Head of State, Edgar Chagwa Lungu appointed Electoral Commission of Zambia Chair Irene Mambilima as Chief Justice. The respected and likeable Mambilima was already substantive Deputy Chief Justice, seconded to the Electoral Commission of Zambia where she did a stellar job.

In retiring Madam Justice Chibesakunda who had served as acting Chief Justice for three years, President Lungu recognised the outgoing judge's contribution to public service by giving her full retirement benefits. Once again the new president found a sensible solution to a problem that had been unnecessarily allowed to fester by his predecessor.

Unfortunately, unforced errors were not confined to constitutional and political matters; they extended to economic affairs as well.

On 23 January, 2012, the government decided to rebase the Zambian Kwacha. Ostensibly they did this in response to a recommendation by the central bank. But the idea of rebasing was also popular in some political circles outside the Bank of Zambia. The rebasing was achieved by knocking off three zeroes from existing banknotes. Thus the old K50, 000 note became K50 under the new currency. The lower value denominations of K500, K100, and K50 were divided by 1000 and converted into coins.

The basic reason advanced for rebasing the currency was that the cost associated with an accumulated loss in the value of the national currency arising from years of high inflation in the 1990s had to be addressed. It was certainly true that the high levels of inflation in the 1990s inconvenienced people who were obliged to carry large quantities of money for what the central bank described as 'relatively low value transactions.'

The government further argued that given the stability of the Zambian currency over the past fifteen years, it was appropriate to rebase and increase the portability of the currency. For most of the time prior to rebasing the currency, the value of the Zambian Kwacha to the US dollar was between 4,800 and 5000. The new rate was thus set at five kwacha to one US dollar.

Sadly, subsequent government policies did nothing to enhance the Kwacha's stability. On the contrary, ill-advised expenditure by the government severely undermined the currency. These decisions included raising presidential emoluments, increasing by astronomical amounts the salaries of public servants, and publishing a badly drafted statutory instrument that had the effect of discouraging foreign investors who feared that the Zambian government was about to reintroduce foreign exchange controls.

On October 08, 2013 the government announced a significant increase in President Michael Sata's salary. According to Statutory Instrument 91 of 2013 the president's salary rose from K 327,000 ($65,400) to K 414,406 (approximately US$ 82,880) per annum. This represented a 79 per cent increase in pay. But the increase was actually higher because the statutory interest also gave the president a special allowance of K108, 934 (about US$21,780.) The last pay increase for the president was in 2012. This increase was with effect from September 01, 2013. The Vice President and other cabinet ministers also had their salaries increased by the same percentage.

In contrast, nurses and midwives were unable to persuade the government to give them an increase greater than four per cent. According to the *Lusaka Times*, nurses and midwives considered the offer of four per cent to be 'a mockery and an insult.' While inconvenienced by the strike that followed the rejection of the offer, members of the public generally empathised with the health workers.

The public saw for themselves when they visited hospitals and health centres how overworked nurses were. The standard that a nurse should attend to eight to ten patients a day had long been dispensed with. The reality in 2013 was that a nurse would be expected to attend to as many as 80 patients in one day.

In early December 2013, the government responded to the strike by firing more than 250 nurses and midwives based at the University Teaching Hospital and Levy Mwanawasa Hospital in Lusaka, Kasama General Hospital, and Livingstone General Hospital. The Minister for Health explained the dismissals to Parliament in typical PF language. According to the Honourable Minister this action would serve as "a lesson to other workers."

In claiming that despite the mass firings, normal operations had been restored at all affected hospitals, the minister underplayed the impact of his government's action.

The nurses' demand of a 100 per cent salary increment, equal pay for equal work, additional patient allowance, K2,000 ($320) monthly housing allowance and K2,000 night duty allowance, may sound excessive but was actually reasonable in the context of the huge salary increases given to the president and his cabinet ministers. It should also be remembered that Zambian nurses have been historically underpaid. In any event the nurses did not expect to get all that they were asking for. A negotiation in good faith could have seen the nurses accepting substantially less than they were claiming. The four per cent pay increase offered by the government was not however realistic.

The dismissal of the nurses alarmed many citizens because of the country's well known shortage of medical staff. The health worker shortage issue was examined in detail in an article written by Jeff Gow, Gavin George, Given Mutinta, Sylvia Mwamba, and Lutungu Ingombe. The article concludes that the 2005 ten year strategic plan for health human resource development has not arrested the shortage of nurses. In fact in 2009 there was a shortage of 28,000 registered and enrolled nurses. According to the *Zambian Economist* progress was made in 2012 to recruit more people, but the country was still 24,000 short of meeting World Health Organisation recommended human resource support.

Zambia has 0.7 nurses per 1000 population and 0.2 midwives per 1000 population. By way of contrast the reader may be interested to know that Denmark has 17 nurses and midwives per 1000 population while India has 1.7 and the United Kingdom has 8.8 (*World Bank*). In light of these damning statistics, many reasonable people saw the firing of nurses as entirely unhelpful.

The populist government too saw the harm being done and reversed its position a year later and reinstated the nurses and other health workers. According to the *Daily Mail* edition of December 19, 2014, the government reinstated all the 570 nurses and health workers fired in December 2013. The government also confirmed that the nurses and health workers reinstated would not lose any of their employment benefits.

In contrast, no public discourse accompanied the increase in pay for politicians. The reason for this lies in a significant law whose passage was largely ignored in the country. In 2009 the Ministerial and Parliamentary Offices (Emoluments) Act was amended so as to remove responsibility for ministerial and parliamentary emoluments from parliament to the minister of finance. The amendment is contained in Section two of the Act and reads as follows:

> There shall be paid to the holder of an office specified in the Schedule such salary and allowances as the Minister responsible for finance may prescribe, by statutory instrument, in consultation with the Standing Orders Committee of the National Assembly.

Thus the pay for cabinet ministers and deputy ministers is now set by the minister of finance without necessary input from parliament. The same is true with respect to the pay of the vice president, the Speaker, the Leader of the Opposition and many other office holders.

Although this change was brought by the MMD government, the PF appears to have been the principal beneficiary of the new law. The US based Zambian academic Professor Henry Kyambalesa has attempted a comparison in emoluments expenditure between the MMD and PF governments. Since the comparison starts in 2008, before the promulgation of the Ministerial and Parliamentary Offices (Emoluments) (Amendment) Act, 2009, the gulf in spending between the two governments cannot be attributed solely to the offensive legislation. The comparison is nonetheless useful in demonstrating the cost of PF style populism.

In 2008, the MMD Government spent a total of K 8,311,182,428 on emoluments of cabinet ministers and deputy ministers. A cabinet minister at that time received a salary of K 75,117,124, a special allowance of K 26,382,673, and a utility allowance of K 26,680,000, for a total monetary package of K 128,179,797. Since there were 24 cabinet ministers, the total spent on these particular office holders (in the old currency) was K 3,076,315,128. That represents a US dollar bill of 640,899 at the then exchange rate.

Deputy Ministers, whose constitutional role is not clear, cost the treasury K 5, 234,867,300. Each one of the 43 deputy ministers received a salary of K 70,953,196 a special allowance of K 24,107,904 and a utility allowance of K 26, 680,000. The total emolument figure for this particular group of office holders was K 5,234,867,300 or US$1,090,597. The total expenditure for both cabinet ministers and deputy ministers was K8, 311,182,428 or US$1,731,496

In contrast the PF spent a total of K 15,964,794,861 or US$ 3,325,998 on the emoluments of cabinet ministers and deputy ministers.

Not only did politicians' emoluments rise astronomically under the Sata presidency but the number of beneficiaries rose too. Although the number of cabinet ministers was reduced to 20, the PF government increased the number of deputy ministers to 53.

The huge increase in the emoluments of largely unproductive public office holders must have contributed to the decline of the national currency that followed. Let us remember that the pay increases extended to office holders other than cabinet ministers and deputy ministers. Statutory Instrument No 92 of 2013 also resulted in huge pay increases for the vice president, the Speaker of the National Assembly, the deputy Speaker, the chief whip, the Leader of the Opposition, the deputy chief whip and committee deputy chairpersons. Taking into account the fact that the national assembly has no fewer than 17 committees, we can easily add another US$ 862,333 to the political emoluments bills.

Inevitably the increase in the emoluments of persons with a huge appetite for foreign goods and services increased pressure on the local currency so that by May 2014 the

Zambian Kwacha was already being described as Africa's worst performing currency (*Zambia Reports.*) This was in spite of the efforts of Bank of Zambia Governor, Michael Gondwe, who was later in the year recognised as Central Bank Governor of the year at the Africa Investments and Business Forum Awards in Washington D.C.

The weakness of the Kwacha was a result of increased government expenditure which also had the effect of negating Michael Gondwe's significant steps of tightening monetary policy by (for example) raising the policy rate and reserve requirements for banks. This was certainly the view of the International Monetary Fund whose resident representative, Tobias Rasmussen, noted in early May 2014 that the kwacha had weakened to be one of the two worst performing currencies in Africa. It did not help that the price of copper, Zambia's main export, was also falling. But this should have been a reason for restraint, not extravagance, on the part of the authorities.

While in Opposition in 2008, President Sata had attacked former President Rupiah Banda over salaries paid to politicians, accusing the then president of 'selfishness.' It is too bad Mr. Sata never followed his own advice once in office.

The reader will recall that when the Kwacha was rebased, currency stability was cited as a reason for the rebasing exercise. The rate was set at 5 new Kwacha to 1 United States dollar. The expectation was that for the foreseeable future the rate would change only marginally. Few would have predicted that the Kwacha would fall from the 5 to 1 rate in January 2012 to 7.6 to 1 in March 2015, representing 52 per cent devaluation in just three years. Matters got worse by November 2015 as the Kwacha traded at 14 to 1.

By the end of the first quarter of 2016 however a combination of tight monetary policy and domestic tax obligations by mining companies (which required them to exchange foreign currency for the Kwacha) improved the performance of the Kwacha as it went from one of the world's worst performers in 2015 to the best in 2016. The Kwacha's performance according to South Africa's *Business Day* issue of April 15, 2016, outshone gold, silver and 150 other currencies and precious metals tracked by Bloomberg. In fact the once beleaguered currency advanced 19.9% against the US dollar in 2016, surpassing gold's 16.3% gain.

As long as government expenditure is kept under control and the power crisis is appropriately addressed, the Kwacha could continue on its upward trend and stabilize in short order, making the country all the more attractive for investment. The challenges to the government include management of the estimated $160 million annual fuel and power subsidy (*Zambia Business Times*, April 24, 2016.) It remains to be seen whether the government will have the courage to end this subsidy.

CHAPTER NINE

Friends and Allies

The Sata who entered State House in 2011 may have been a shadow of the old fiery action leader who had so impressed the nation when he served as mayor of Lusaka during the One Party era, and subsequently as minister of health after the reintroduction of democracy; but two things remained constant between the old and the new Sata. Both had a deep sense of loyalty and survival.

Sata associated himself with unlikely characters out of a sense of loyalty, misplaced admiration, or the belief that potential enemies should be appeased before they strike. This may explain why Sata went out of his way to court Kenneth Kaunda who at the time of the PF victory was universally discredited as a poor economics manager, although he was revered by many for simply being the first Zambian President.

Although Sata abandoned Kaunda's socialist party in 1991 to join the more economically liberal Movement for Multiparty Democracy, Sata was never an advocate of unfettered free enterprise. Like Kaunda, he understood the political benefit of state control of the economy. But for the fact that by the time Sata came along democracy and free enterprise were too entrenched in Zambia to be reversed, he would probably have renationalised some key industries including the mining sector. There would never have been wholesale nationalisation under Sata who had spent many years in the private sector and had some respect for the free market, but some private companies would have been repossessed by the state.

During the ten years that the party spent in opposition, there were advocates of renationalisation within the PF. These people also tended to support the idea of reintroducing foreign exchange controls.

Kenneth Kaunda certainly found the prospect of re-establishing state companies quite attractive. He often lamented the disappearance of "my companies", as he affectionately referred to the failed state enterprises.

Fortunately for Zambia, Sata understood that renationalising the mining sector in 2011 would simply not work but instead would attract such negative international commentary as to guarantee a severe foreign direct investment drought for a long time.

About four years before the PF came to power, I responded to calls for renationalisation of the mining sector by a future PF government by arranging a meeting between two senior executives of a Canadian mining company known for its ethical business practices, and Mr. Michael Chilufya Sata. Mr. Sata arrived on the dot for the meeting and in typical fashion quickly went on to verbally mock his interlocutors by describing them as 'infesters', a play on the word 'investors'.

Despite the banter, the meeting was successful because on this occasion Mr. Sata was prepared to listen and to learn. He left the meeting impressed with the Canadian company's commitment to corporate social responsibility in Zambia. My subsequent discussions with Sata suggested he had understood that Zambia could get all the benefits of having a thriving mining industry without the headaches that came with ownership.

By the time Sata became President, renationalising any part of the Zambian economy was seen universally as untenable. This would have been a disappointment to the dictatorial Mr. Kaunda who continued to see the days of inefficient and corrupt state companies as the glory days of Zambia.

But it must have been something of a consolation prize for Kenneth Kaunda when Sata announced during his New Year address at the end of 2013, his government's intention to establish a new state enterprise to be known as the Industrial Development Corporation as a tool to allegedly modernise and diversify the economy. The IDC was incorporated under the Companies Act on January 23, 2014 with a paid up capital of K20 million (US$ 2.7 Million).

Precisely what this company was going to do remained a mystery for a while and many feared it was just going to be an additional parasitic encumbrance on the structure of companies still owned by the state. As far as could be ascertained, this entity would have no capacity to generate its own revenue. On December 14, 2015 the pro government *Times of Zambia* offered a rationale for the company.

According to the paper, the closure of the Zambia Industrial and Mining Corporation and other key corporations such as the old Industrial Development Corporation (later known as INDECO) and the Financial Development Corporation (FINDECO) in the 1990s, had left state owned enterprises under the direct supervision of line ministries within Government. The challenge with this arrangement was that line ministries lacked the requisite commercial and investment expertise and resources needed to ensure the positive performance of the state enterprises under their supervision.

The newspaper went on to explain that the corporation was "established to own and manage these investments on a commercial basis, allowing the ministries of finance, commerce, trade and industry and all other to focus on policy making." This statement would offer some comfort but for the fact that the corporation is chaired by the republican president 'for the purpose of protecting the national interest.' The national interest, we can be sure would be as determined by the president. This guarantees a repeat of the deleterious politicization that doomed the state enterprises of yesteryear.

It is certainly a good idea to provide a commercial umbrella for existing state enterprises and deliver them from line ministry supervision. But this role can be played by the government investment arm, ZCCM-IH, which is run along commercial lines and which already has stakes in key mining companies. ZCCM-IH does not confine itself to the mining sector and has already entered some of the sectors targeted by IDC.

It is not unreasonable to conclude that the ill-conceived Industrial Development Corporation was established simply to appease Mr. Kaunda and others still stuck in socialist dogma. If so, this would represent a remarkable example of the lengths Sata would have gone to appease allies and friends.

Besides loyalty there was another reason why Sata wanted to keep Kaunda close to him. The relevant history here is that in 2006, prior to that year's presidential elections, Kenneth Kaunda declared Michael Sata unfit for the presidency. Kaunda based this observation on his past experience working with Sata. But as has been seen, Kaunda abandoned this unflattering view of Sata soon after the latter won the presidency. Sata had reached out to Kaunda and promised him recognition and financial support. Why was Sata so keen to have Kaunda in his camp?

In post-Independence Zambia, politicians have relied heavily on the roles they played in the fight against colonialism, for their legitimacy. Sata was no exception. He frequently projected himself as a freedom fighter. In fact this claim is at best misleading, as Sishuwa D Sishuwa, the Oxford based political science scholar who has studied Sata's rise to power, has suggested. At the height of the nationalist struggle for independence from the United Kingdom when Kenneth Kaunda and other colleagues like Simon Kapwepwe, Malama Sokoni, and Nalumino Mundia were fighting for freedom and experiencing harassment by the colonial regime, Sata served as a constable in the colonial police service. Being a member of the Mobile Unit that was used regularly to quell political protest, he often found himself on the opposite side of nationalist leaders. In other words, his role as a colonial operative brought him in direct confrontation with the freedom fighters. Sata would later quit the colonial police and join the trade union movement which was affiliated with the nationalists. But that was in 1962 and the damage to his reputation may already have been done. He was already resented by many in UNIP nationalist circles and viewed as a collaborator. His supporters would point out that while in the colonial service, Sata in fact gave invaluable information to the nationalists. This claim has never been conclusively proven. But even if this were the case, Sata could still never really be a true freedom fighter like Humphrey Mulemba or Sikota Wina or any of the other acknowledged freedom heroes, simply because he was not in the nationalist trenches at the critical time.

Sishuwa suggests this history is important in understanding Sata's obsession with rehabilitating Kaunda and building close ties with him. By associating so publicly with Kaunda, an undoubted champion of the freedom struggle, Sata was making a self-conscious and belated attempt to re-assert his credentials as a freedom fighter. He also wanted to distinguish himself from his political enemy Frederick Chiluba who while serving as president was seen by many as unkind to Kaunda.

Sata was keen to erase the memory of his service as a colonial police operative and therefore a collaborator who undermined the freedom fight, and to win acceptance or admittance to the increasingly exclusive nationalist club of real freedom fighters.

Giving Kaunda the political stage he so obviously craved, also won the silence of the former head of state who was now less likely to comment negatively about Sata's role in the colonial police service.

This is not to suggest that Sata was mercenary. He was not. He was an authoritarian leader with a strong sense of loyalty to the country. He valued order, sometimes at the expense of good judgment, as evidenced by his willingness to serve in the colonial police service.

Sata saw these qualities in Kaunda as well. Readers familiar with Kenneth Kaunda's history may recall that as a student at Munali Secondary School Kaunda relished the nickname Hitler. The sobriquet was not employed entirely out of ignorance but also out of admiration for Adolph Hitler. The respected author, educationist, and lawyer John Mupanga Mwanakatwe researched the matter for his book *End of Kaunda Era* and found evidence to show that Kaunda had indeed admired Hitler. One reliable source who confirmed this was the astute but unassuming freedom fighter Malama John Sokoni. Like Kaunda, Mr. Sokoni was born, bred, and largely educated in Chinsali. As Kaunda's childhood friend, Sokoni knew what he was talking about.

Furthermore, it is now a matter of record that during the 1990 Gulf crisis Kaunda expressed great admiration for Saddam Hussein, another enthusiast of brutal order, whom he described as "my good brother". He must have been a good brother indeed because Kaunda also named a major boulevard in the Zambian capital after the Iraqi dictator. The boulevard was renamed Los Angeles Boulevard when the country reverted to democracy.

Sata may not have admired Hitler but he did understand authority and the importance of maintaining order. His own nickname was King Cobra, after the large venomous and territorial snake. But admiration for authority figures or even the belief that potential enemies should be appeased were not always considerations in the friendships President Sata chose to nurture.

For example, the overwhelming reason for Sata's support of Ms. Lombe Chibesakunda as Chief Justice of Zambia appears to be based largely on loyalty. The fact that Ms. Chibesakunda is a competent woman would have been a bonus.

Loyalty also appears to be the central reason for President Sata's relationship with Xavier Chungu.

When the Movement for Multiparty Democracy won the first democratic poll in 23 years, a decision was taken to appoint a relatively junior officer as head of the Zambia Security Intelligence Service. This was seen as the best way of making a clean break from the Kaunda era. The new head of intelligence was Xavier Franklin Chungu. Michael Sata was very much involved in this appointment.

Chungu went on serve for a decade before the new president, Levy Patrick Mwanawasa, relieved him of his duties.

When Mwanawasa mounted his targeted campaign against corruption, Chungu and President Chiluba with several other former government officials were accused of stealing more than US $40 million from Zambian Government coffers while in office. Investigators believed at the time that the former president and his inner circle which included Chungu diverted state funds into privately held bank accounts abroad.

In June 2004, while court proceedings were taking place and investigations continuing, Xavier Chungu jumped bail and fled the country.

Chungu did return to Zambia four years later and was re-arrested at the Lusaka International Airport. Things were nevertheless beginning to look up for the former intelligence chief. Mwanawasa had died and been replaced by a more agreeable president, Rupiah Bwezani Banda. In subsequent court proceedings, Chungu was cleared of many of the charges against him. In what seemed like a show of appreciation, Chungu decided to campaign for President Banda ahead of the September 20, 2011 general election. Banda lost that election to Michael Sata.

Given this background, many observers of Zambian politics were surprised that on October 31, 2011 President Sata appointed Xavier Chungu as permanent secretary of Luapula Province. The appointment caused outrage, with a personal friend of Sata's (who was not in government) going to State House to berate the president publically. There were other voices of protest including the First Lady's, and in the end the appointment was rescinded.

Why did Sata make this appointment? He must have known it would be controversial. It would certainly be unpopular with the foot soldiers that were challenged by Chungu as he campaigned for Sata's opponent. The concerns of the foot soldiers however would not weigh heavily on Sata's mind. Michael Chilufya Sata was not one to bear a grudge. Despite his authoritarian nature, Sata forgave easily, as evidenced by the number of former political foes that he embraced throughout his career.

The reason for his embrace of Chungu lies in the late president's deep sense of loyalty.

On the 17th of April 2002, Michael Chilufya Sata, was charged with the offence of theft of two government-owned vehicles. The following day Sata appeared before Lusaka resident magistrate, Frank Tembo to deny the two counts of theft.

Sata's trial date was set for April 23, but since bail is no longer possible in cases involving theft of motor vehicles, under amendments made to the law during the Chiluba era, Sata was obliged to go back to remand prison until his matter was disposed of.

Sata's arrest followed a directive to police by the minister of works and supply, Ludwig Sondashi, to investigate arrest and charge Sata for converting government property to his personal use. Sata and Sondashi had been colleagues in the Chiluba government until Sata resigned his office of Minister without Portfolio after Chiluba had sidestepped him as presidential successor in favour of Levy Mwanawasa.

Responding to the arrest, Sata claimed, "This is just the beginning of my political persecution. But I am ready to fight it to the bitter end..." Indeed many observers saw this as harassment of Sata by the Mwanawasa government. The mood generated by this general perception perhaps made it easier for Xavier Chungu to help his old benefactor.

Although Chungu was no longer head of the Zambian security service, he was on cordial terms with his successor, Reggie Phiri, and others in the organisation. The new Director of Intelligence was able to produce a letter purportedly written by Chungu and authorising Sata to use the vehicles in question. Many observers of Zambian politics believe the letter was backdated. Nonetheless, the evidence adduced put

Sata in the role of an operative who needed the vehicle for undercover operations. With respect to one motor vehicle, Chungu testified that around the year 2000, the Office of the President acquired a Toyota Land Cruiser GX from Toyota Zambia and "the motor vehicle was later given to Mr. Michael Sata in his personal capacity as a friend to the system."

Far from being a thief of motor vehicles, the former policeman was cast as a legitimate user of government transportation who in so doing enhanced the security of the country.

Sata was acquitted on the 14th of May 2002.

Sata was subjected to a great deal of indignity during this ordeal. And yet it never occurred to him when he became president to seek revenge on Ludwig Sondashi, the architect of the charges. Sondashi, who had in the meantime been dismissed from the Mwanawasa government, certainly appreciated this.

Campaigning for his new party in preparation for the January 20, 2015 presidential by election, Mr. Sondashi told a public rally at President's Park in Chinsali that Mr. Sata had been "a selfless leader who should be emulated by all Zambians."

It has been suggested that Sata's loyalty did not extend to those who supported him financially. In this regard the claim has been made (with justification) that after winning the presidency Sata ignored some of the people who had raised significant amounts of money for his campaign. Sata probably did this out of fear that his more astute financial backers may claim a role in government and if he let them in they would either thwart his agenda or outshine him. Where no such danger existed, Sata maintained his loyalty.

My dear Rajan

One example of a financial backer who benefitted from Sata's sense of loyalty was Rajan Mahtani.

Rajan Lekhraj Mahtani was born in Ndola, the capital of the Zambian Copperbelt Province, on the 14th of February 1948. His parents were British protected Northern Rhodesians of Indian descent. For many years they ran a supermarket in the centre of the city. In the early days however Rajan's mother, Mohini Mahtani, was not visibly active in the running of the family business.

Mahtani Junior did his primary education in Ndola before being sent to Kwekwe in Southern Rhodesia (now Zimbabwe) for high school. The school was founded by the Marist Brothers, a religious institute founded in turn by St. Marcellin Champagnat, and dedicated "to make Jesus Christ known and loved" through the education of young people.

Mahtani, who was born a Hindu, converted to Catholicism and assumed the name Roger while studying at the Marist Brothers School. He returned to his home country of Zambia after obtaining his Ordinary level school certificate.

Rajan Mahtani's early life was not without trauma and tragedy. His youngest sibling Girdhari committed suicide in the basement of the supermarket operated by his parents. Mahtani Senior himself died while Rajan was still a teenager. It was at this time that Mrs. Mohini Mahtani became more visible as a manager of the business. She seemed to spend her entire time at the till dressed in a white sari, and had a reputation for unpleasantness. Few customers enjoyed her company.

Mrs. Mahtani must have suffered greatly not only from the loss of her husband but also the premature death of her youngest son. Later her older son too would die, but this time from malaria.

Rajan too must have suffered greatly from these events. While the outcomes of childhood sibling loss are unpredictable, this kind of tragedy always has consequences. Typically these consequences are negative, such as feelings of guilt. But the consequences are not uniformly and consistently negative. Indeed, according to Dr P.G. White (*Long Term Effects of Childhood Sibling Loss*) the outcomes of childhood sibling loss can sometimes be positive. For example, survivor siblings can experience psychological growth as a result of the tragedy. In a study conducted by Dr White, survivors observed that their priorities about life had changed and they appreciated life more now that they had greater emotional strength. Other positive benefits identified were increased independence and the need and opportunity to examine religious beliefs.

It is perhaps in this context that Mahtani's conversion to Christianity while at school in Zimbabwe is best understood. In later life Mahtani also enjoyed being creative, as evidenced by the number and nature of business ventures he got involved in. This is consistent with research showing that some individuals respond to their loss by becoming even more creative.

But while these outcomes may be positive for the survivor sibling they are not necessarily employed in a way that is beneficial for society.

Rajan Mahtani enjoys power and prestige. He is a Fellow of the Chartered Association of Certified Accountants and also claims to hold a PhD in 'Commercial Law' from London University, as he informed me. He has however informed other people that his PhD is from the London Institute of Business Studies.

If Mahtani does indeed have a PhD, he must have employed near superhuman powers to study for the degree because at the material time he was busy running his accounting practice, acquiring interests in all manner of corporations for his holding company, setting up a leasing company and finally establishing Finance Bank. The second point to note about Mr. Mahtani's degree is that 'Commercial Law' would be too broad a topic for a PhD thesis. The following is an example of a PhD thesis title from the European University Institute:

> Competition and integration - what goals count? : EEC competition law and goals of industrial, monetary, and cultural policy.

Whether or not Mr. Mahtani is the holder of a legitimate PhD from a recognised university, it is important for him to be addressed as 'Dr Mahtani.' In this regard he is in distinguished company among his countrymen, many of whom have resorted to buying degrees from unaccredited American universities for the purpose of enjoying the same honorific title.

Mahtani's critics accuse him of having a craving for attention that is greater than most people's. According to these critics Mahtani is not content to simply being a well-known successful businessman, he also wants to publicise his spiritual credentials as a born again Christian. Mahtani's Christmas Day 2012 visit to Kamfinsa Prison on the outskirts of the City of Kitwe to deliver a sermon to inmates is usually given as an example of this craving for attention. During that visit

Mahtani authoritatively assured the prisoners of God's imminent help, urging them to imitate Joseph in the Bible.

It will be recalled that Mahtani converted to Christianity as a very young person. He could not have known at that time that being a Christian could bring rewards in the form of positive publicity to feed the alleged craving for attention. Had that been Mahtani's intent he would surely have developed a career much earlier as an evangelical preacher. Mahtani is a meticulous man with a penchant for detailed planning. Had Mahtani intended to use Christianity purely for egotistical reasons, he would have done a much better job of managing this aspect of his life.

I have no doubt that Mahtani is a sincere Christian with a desire to do good deeds. He certainly has his faults but faking Christianity is not one of them. He is a believer whose closest family member is his sister Mary who is married to a respected pastor. Mary and her husband are devout Christians.

This persona is in marked contrast to the image of Mahtani as a ruthless businessman. As a young lawyer in Ndola I recall many Italian business people who were terrified and resentful of Mahtani. Most of these business people were neither Zambian citizens nor permanent residents and according to the laws and practices of the day could not conduct business freely. They often needed a Zambian partner to comply with the many requirements of running a business. It certainly helped to have on the board of directors a Zambian with good connections to the government.

The common complaint against Mahtani was his alleged ability to trick business owners into surrendering control of their ventures to his holding company. This would typically be preceded by an offer of help in the form of loans and other financial support. In due course these loans would mount into significant debt, not repayable immediately. It was at this point that Mahtani would strike and convert the loans and advances into shareholding, at the most favourable terms possible for his holding company. This is allegedly how Mahtani built his impressive business empire.

That he is a shrewd businessman is beyond question. What is questionable are his ethics. He is said to be good at dressing up diabolical schemes in respectable clothing. But on many occasions when Mahtani's alleged victims came to my practice for help, we found ourselves unable to prove fraud even as we understood clearly that the client believed a wrong had been perpetrated. We were however able to help potential future victims by giving appropriate advice before they sought financial help from him or anyone else for their fledgling ventures.

Mahtani has also calculated that a successful business empire cannot be built without political connections. For this reason, Mahtani has cultivated a close relationship with all Zambian presidents, starting with Kenneth Kaunda. But this is not unusual. During the Kaunda era almost every successful businessman calculated a good relationship with the regime or members of the head of state's family.

The main challenge for businesses operating in Zambia during the Kaunda years was access to foreign exchange in the context of a rigorous exchange control regime that restricted capital outflows from Zambia. Businesses that needed to import goods and services had to apply for permission from the government for an allocation of foreign currency to facilitate the purchase of what they needed from abroad. The decision to allocate foreign exchange to a particular business was not always determined by market forces but rather by political considerations. In general Mahtani's businesses were viewed favourably by the Kaunda government and so they tended to be accommodated. But sometimes business people needed more than Kaunda and his inefficient system of allocating foreign exchange could offer. So they flouted exchange control regulations by externalising money illegally. Kaunda believed that Mahtani was engaging in this behaviour and in 1980 ordered the detention without trial of Rajan Mahtani. Kaunda was not able to prove any of the allegations against Mahtani. But the lack of proof would not stand in the way of Kaunda's wishes to imprison the businessman because in those days Zambia was under a state of emergency that (like Hitler's *Law of Authorisation*) allowed the head of state to imprison anyone without charge or trial.

The relationship between Kaunda and Mahtani did eventually improve. In April 2014, Mahtani hosted a lavish 90th birthday party for the former dictator. The event took place six days before the actual birthday on April 28, and was attended by a select group of dignitaries including Mahtani's mother, Mohini, who had flown in for the occasion from London where she now lived. She was dressed in white but despite her advanced age appeared more cheerful than she had done looking after the family business in Ndola all those years ago.

At this time Kenneth Kaunda had of course ceased to be president of Zambia. His fall had come in October 1991 when Frederick Chiluba won the first democratic elections in 23 years and became president. Mahtani had sensed as soon as the country's constitution was amended with a view to reintroducing democracy that Chiluba would win the ensuing poll. He therefore gave substantial financial support to Chiluba and his political party.

Thus the relationship between the new democratically elected president and Mahtani started off on a good footing. But this cordial relationship would soon end.

On 3 June 1998 Rajan Mahtani was arrested. Five days later he was charged with treason and broadly accused of involvement in an alleged coup attempt eight months earlier. Prior to these charges Mahtani had been removed as executive chairman of Finance Bank, the jewel in the crown of his business empire. It was believed that political pressure had been brought on the bank to distance itself from its founding chairman. Since Kaunda's state of emergency had been ended with the return of democracy, and Chiluba could not get away with more than a month of emergency powers, Mahtani had to be charged with a non bailable offence in order to secure his confinement. He was charged with treason. It is doubtful that Mahtani was involved in any enterprise to overthrow the democratically elected government of Zambia. The accusations themselves and the subsequent behaviour of the authorities suggest that these charges were fabricated.

The statement of offence against Mahtani alleged that:

Between July 1, 1995 and October 28, 1998 in Lusaka jointly and whilst acting together with others unknown you conspired to overthrow by unlawful means the Government of the Republic of Zambia.

The statement of offence was remarkably vague for an indictment of this seriousness. If Mahtani had been involved in a criminal enterprise for a period of three years, why had the authorities not arrested him earlier? Also, if the persons Mahtani was conspiring with were unknown, how did the authorities know there was a conspiracy at all?

One of the persons detained with Mahtani was the late Princess Nakatindi, a member of the western Zambian aristocracy who, together with her husband the veteran politician Sikota Wina, had given much support to Chiluba in his quest for the presidency. She testified at Mahtani's writ of habeas corpus application hearing that 'all the monies that I am alleged to have received from former Finance Bank executive Rajan Mahtani were specifically meant for business and not for the purpose of overthrowing the government.' That was credible evidence given that the Winas did run businesses at that time.

Evidently, the government itself had no better evidence than this because six weeks after his incarceration, Mahtani was released by a Lusaka High Court judge following the state's decision to enter a *nolle prosequi* which basically meant that the state had no evidence to support the prosecution.

The relationship between Frederick Chiluba and Rajan Mahtani never regained its cordiality. Chiluba had at least two basic reasons for being disappointed with Mahtani. The first had to do with what is known in Zambia as 'the Carlington Maize Scam.' Early in the Chiluba presidency, Zambia suffered a food shortage on account of insufficient rainfall. A decision was therefore made to buy maize from outside the country in order to make up for the shortfall in the staple food. It was agreed that the maize would be supplied by a Canadian based outfit called Carlington Sales Company.

Mahtani got involved in the proposal to source maize from Carlington and travelled to Canada for this purpose. When he got there, Mahtani presented himself as economic advisor to President Chiluba and thus gave himself the authority to "arrange the contract," a task that reportedly earned him $240,000. Chiluba subsequently claimed that he had been concerned at the price Mahtani and Carlington Sales Company expected Zambia to pay for the maize. The price was high partly because it took into account the handsome commission paid to Mahtani. The profit margin built into the price was so high that low income Zambians would find it difficult if not impossible to buy the corn flour ground from this maize when it eventually arrived in the country. Chiluba was reportedly incensed that Mahtani would make so much profit at the expense of poor Zambians.

It is not clear why Mahtani should have been paid anything at all because Zambia's Food Reserve Agency which would be responsible for transactions like this had assigned the maize contract to Nedcor Bank of South Africa, who actually signed the contract with Carlington in 1998. As the former Food Reserve Agency CEO, Chance Kabaghye, has testified, all Mahtani did was to introduce Ali Ben Menashe, the owner of Carlington Sales Company of Canada to Zambia.

To add insult to injury, the maize was never actually delivered to Zambia. For this reason the Zambian attorney general, Bonaventure Mutale, took the matter to the London Court of International Arbitration with a view to recovering monies already paid under the $24 million contract.

On October 31, 2001 the London Court of International Arbitration ordered Carlington Sales Company to pay Zambia's Food Reserve Agency $6.1 million plus eight percent interest as money owed to FRA for Carlington's failure to deliver 50,000 metric tonnes of maize to the agency. The court further ordered Carlington to pay legal costs in the amount of £334,651 in sterling. It is noteworthy that reparations were not sought against Mahtani and the court ordered none.

Another reason Chiluba was unhappy with Mahtani related to the establishment of Finance Bank in Malawi. Knowing that Chiluba had a good relationship with President Elson Bakili Muluzi of Malawi, Mahtani begged Chiluba for an introduction to the Malawian president. Mahtani felt that he needed the introduction to help him secure a banking licence in Malawi. Chiluba obliged and in due course Mahtani did open a subsidiary of Finance Bank in that country.

On 17 May, 2005, after a banking presence of ten years in the country, the Reserve Bank of Malawi suspended Finance Bank's foreign currency licence after carrying out investigations which went back to 1999. The Reserve Bank went further and also revoked the banking licence for Finance Bank accusing it of unsound methods and illegal externalisation of foreign exchange, the same charge Kaunda had made in Zambia when he imprisoned Mahtani without trial in 1980.

The central bank had been investigating Mahtani for years and it would appear Muluzi had called Chiluba prior to commencement of investigations to complain about Mahtani and to remind the Zambian president that the banking licence had been issued on the basis of Chiluba's recommendation.

This would explain more credibly the tension between Chiluba and Mahtani than vague allegations about Mahtani's involvement in a coup plot.

Despite falling out with Chiluba, Mahtani continued to have a good relationship with Levy Mwanawasa, the vice president of Chiluba's party who had also previously served as republican vice president.

It must have been a godsend for Mahtani when (after serving the maximum of two presidential terms permissible under the constitution) Chiluba asked Mwanawasa to be the MMD party standard bearer in the election of 2001. Mahtani was only too eager to help his friend and former lawyer and fellow Ndola citizen with cash donations.

When Mwanawasa became president, Mahtani found himself with a reliable friend in State House. His businesses flourished as did his influence. Sometimes the influence was used quite crudely.

The case of Zambezi Oil and Transport Company is quite instructive in this regard. In my book *Getting Zambia to Work* I make reference to a petroleum company that was illegally allowed to locate alongside a busy Ndola highway next to power lines. ZOT was the company in question. From this unsafe location the subsidiary of Tanganyika Investments Oil and Transport dealt in inflammable petroleum products.

In 2004, a UK company - Lukoil International Trading and Supply Company (LITASCO), sued ZOT for an outstanding debt of $2.6 million in the Lusaka High Court.

ZOT took the position that LITASCO's claim, if any, should be against Tanganyika Investments Oil and another outfit called Euro Products, the two companies that supplied LITASCO. ZOT was a separate person from its Tanzanian parent.

ZOT was on solid legal ground with respect to this argument. In addition, the contractual provisions that LITASCO was relying on called for settlement of disputes by the London Court of International Arbitration. LITASCO therefore took the matter to London and obtained a default judgment because of ZOT's failure to appear.

There are specific rules that pertain to enforcement of foreign judgements in Zambia. LITASCO did not comply with these requirements and was therefore unable to enforce the judgement locally against ZOT.

In October 2007, Gati Al-Jebouri, LITASCO's Bulgarian born chief executive officer, arranged to meet President Mwanawasa in London. When he returned to Zambia,

Mwanawasa wrote to ZOT's Managing Director urging settlement of LITASCO's claim. As if this were not unseemly enough, Mwanawasa informed the managing director that LITASCO had appointed Mahtani as the firm's consultant in Zambia.

In his role as consultant Mahtani wrote to the Zambian president expressing concern that ZOT's alleged debt was harming Zambia's reputation. Mahtani also explained that he had passed on all relevant legal documents to the President's legal advisor in order to facilitate speedy settlement of the matter.

But ZOT's managing director was not going to be intimidated. He explained to Mwanawasa that the debt in question was incurred by the two Tanzanian companies TIOT and Euro Products. Mwanawasa would of course have known this as a lawyer but out of loyalty to Mahtani he allowed himself to be used as a debt collector. This enhanced neither Mr. Mwanawasa's image nor the Zambian presidency.

Mahtani was not ready to give up however just because ZOTI was not legally indebted to Mahtani's client in London. As he has done on so many other occasions, Mahtani turned to Finance Bank to settle a score.

Like most large companies, ZOT had a bank overdraft facility to help it manage day to day operations. This facility happened to be with Finance Bank. When ZOT management refused to settle the debt owed by its Tanzanian parent and Euro Products, Mahtani called in the overdraft ZOT had with Finance Bank at short notice.

ZOT owed Finance Bank about $560,000 in local currency. This was not a huge amount given that ZOT had fuel stocks with a value of $1.4 million in their reserve tanks and at filling stations. ZOT relied on this in its efforts to persuade Finance

Bank that it had enough assets to cover the overdraft and to get Mahtani to reverse his decision. But Mahtani was not pulling the plug on ZOT because they were a risk; he simply wanted the company to settle a debt payable to his clients but incurred by persons legally different from ZOT.

ZOT now had a week within which to pay the $560,000. Of course they failed to raise the money in such a short period of time. It was at this point that Finance Bank placed ZOT in receivership.

Mahtani was quite visible in the ZOT case. This is not seen by his critics as the usual *modus operandi*. He is seen as a businessman who acts through third parties to avoid personal liability. This could be a simplistic assessment of business transactions that may be too complex for the average person to fathom.

For example, Rajan Mahtani is believed to have influenced the government decision to sell Konkola Copper Mines Plc (KCM) after the departure of Anglo American Corporation whose new leadership in London had unwisely decided to disengage from Zambia and other African countries.

There was a reputable mining company interested in acquiring KCM at market value but the Mwanawasa government was not interested in selling to that particular company despite its excellent credentials. The excuse given by President Mwanawasa when I spoke to him about the matter was that if this company were allowed to acquire KCM, it would become so dominant in the Zambian mining sector that the country would become as dependent on this company as it had been on the departing Anglo American Corporation.

I was disappointed with this decision as I had gone out of my way to interest the reputable company into adding KCM to its existing ventures.

I followed the KCM case reasonably closely, and I have no doubt that in the sale to the Indian owned and London based Vedanta Resources Plc that followed, a huge amount of money was paid 'under the table' to persons connected to the Mwanawasa government. I should say however I never came across convincing evidence that Mwanawasa himself was bribed but I cannot similarly vouch for other people around him, including members of his own family. Equally there is no evidence to show that Mahtani benefited from the transaction as assumed by so many people in Zambia. Nevertheless it is telling that for many the instinct was to turn their eyes to Mahtani as soon as there was a smell of financial impropriety.

Andrew Sardanis has analysed the sale of KCM to Vedanta in some detail in his book *Zambia: The First 50 years*. I wish I could say much of what Sardanis says in his book is farfetched. I cannot. On the contrary, what Sardanis has unearthed may only be the tip of the ice berg.

The details of the sale, which included diminution of shares of Zambia Copper Investments Ltd (ZCI) and Zambia Consolidated Copper Mines-Investment Holdings (ZCCM-IH), are complicated and the reader interested in understanding these details is referred to Chapter 20 of Sardanis' excellent book. For our purposes, suffice it to state that Vedanta itself reported the gross cost of the transaction as only $49.2 million.

As Sardanis has pointed out, not a cent of this paltry sum actually went to the nation. Vedanta obtained 51 per cent control of KCM by subscribing for shares in the amount of $25 million. Accordingly ZCI reduced its interest in KCM from 58 to 28.4 per cent. ZCI received $23.2 million for the diminution of its shareholding. ZCCM-IH then reduced its shareholding from 42 to 20.6 per cent. For this the state corporation should have received a cash payment of $16.8 million.

There is no evidence however that ZCCM-IH was ever paid this amount. But there is a credit note in this amount from the Ministry of Finance in favour of ZCCM-IH against ZCCM-IH's debt to government. The question asked by Sardanis: "Did Mwanawasa waive the payment and not tell the nation...or did the payment go into somebody's pocket...?" is still relevant.

I have heard in mining circles that this amount did indeed go into someone's pocket. There was another unknown amount that was paid in similar fashion after the Zambian government agreed to allow Vedanta to carry forward all the tax losses (amounting to $635,897,000) 'incurred up to and including 31 December 2003'. These tax losses were incurred by the previous owners of Konkola, not by Vedanta.

The question frequently asked is: How could Mwanawasa the champion of the fight against corruption have been so callous with such an important national asset? The allegation I have heard is that most of these arrangements were negotiated by Mahtani and a member of Mwanawasa's family. It is further alleged that Mahtani went on to receive substantial payments as a result of his involvement in the negotiation of such an exceptionally generous deal for Vedanta. He did not however get shares in the mining company. This would represent a departure from Mahtani's usual *modus operandi*, as demonstrated by his involvement in a company called Zambezi Portland Cement.

Antonio Ventriglia and his family arrived in Zambia in 1957 from Italy. They set up a terrazzo company that soon proved successful. Many years later, Antonio and Manuela

Ventriglia decided to branch out into cement manufacturing, and formed Zambezi Portland Cement.

The family asked Rajan Mahtani to arrange financing for the new venture. Mahtani agreed and used Finance Bank to syndicate a loan from, among others, the European Development Fund and the Nairobi based Preferential Trade Area (PTA) Bank.

In return for this help, Mahtani was given a 49 per cent stake in Zambezi Portland Cement. The Ventriglias were not happy with this arrangement but felt they had little option if they were going to secure the US$100 million financing they needed quickly.

It appears however that ZPC may not have had all the financing needed because it soon exhausted its borrowing limit and was again looking to Mahtani for additional help. This time, Mahtani wanted collateral in the form of the very successful terrazzo company, Ital Terrazzo Ltd, which the Ventriglias had started when they first arrived in Zambia.

With this 'help' the company was able to increase plant capacity but this only increased the need for further capital. Mahtani was once again on hand to provide the additional capital. The price this time was a further increase in the shareholding owned by Finsbury Investments Ltd, Mahtani's holding company. He proposed a reduction in the Ventriglia shareholding from 51 % to 42% and a corresponding increase in Mahtani's shareholding from 49 per cent to 58 per cent.

There were attempts to increase further Mahtani's shareholding to 75% but these appear to have come to nothing; but the wrangles between the Ventriglias and Mahtani undermined production, making it impossible for the overleveraged company to service its debts appropriately. Mahtani, now wearing his Finance Bank hat, responded to the company's woes by placing it under receivership. He went further and also placed Ital Terrazzo Ltd. under receivership because earlier Mahtani had insisted that Ital be used as collateral for some of ZPC's loans.

The story of Zambezi Portland Cement and Rajan Mahtani is full of twists and turns involving false criminal complaints against the Ventriglias made by Mahtani and ultimately resulting in their deportation from Zambia, the only country they have known as a family.

The Ventriglias did eventually return to Zambia and by April 2015 had regained control of their company.

On June 02, 2015, Rajan Mahtani was arrested by police in Lusaka and charged with two counts of forgery. The specific allegation was that Mahtani in concert with others had forged documents purporting to transfer 500,000,000 shares from Zambezi Portland Cement to Finsbury Investments Limited. The forgery was alleged to have taken place on 12 December 2006.

In July 2015 the Ventriglia family secured an important legal victory against Mahtani, whom they accused of attempting to steal a majority shareholding in their company. Mahtani had gone to court seeking an injunction to restrain the Ventriglias from acting as shareholders of the company. After reviewing the evidence, Mr. Justice Chanshi found that there was no basis upon which Mahtani could seek such an injunction.

In welcoming Mr. Justice Chanshi's ruling, the management of ZPC hinted that they had been concerned that Mahtani's influence might extend to the judiciary itself. Here is the official management response:

> We welcome the court's ruling on this matter, and we hope that
> the broader business community can continue to benefit from a

return to rule of law and judicial independence in Zambia. Mahtani has acted in a clear criminal fashion with regard to our company, using his influence with the state to steal from successful businesses. For many years, the true owners of Zambezi Portland Cement have suffered hundreds of millions of dollars in damages from the corporate raid and theft by the once-powerful Mr. Mahtani, and we are hoping to put those days behind us.

The sentiments expressed by ZPC management were not a product of fantasy. In 2011 Mahtani was found with a case to answer and put on his defence for forging the signature of the Deputy Governor of the Bank of Zambia. The prosecution was however abruptly terminated when Mr. Sata came to power.

The Director of Prosecutions then was Mutembo Nchito who at the time of writing is being investigated by a specially constituted tribunal for allegedly receiving a bribe of $4.2 million from Mr. Mahtani in exchange for dismissing the case.

Controversial Director of Public Prosecutions, Mutembo Nchinto

To say that Rajan Mahtani is a controversial figure would be an understatement. Undoubtedly some of the negative reputation is deserved. It is also fair to say there are positive aspects of his character that the critical public do not see. For a man who is said to crave publicity, Mahtani has been remarkably low keyed about his philanthropic activities.

For example, the next festive season after his visit to Kamfinsa Prison Mahtani donated money for the welfare of staff and patients at a rural hospital in the Luapula Province. He does seem to have an interest in helping vulnerable citizens. I know from personal experience that he has supported orphanages. He also had an active corporate social responsibility agenda when he served as Chairman of Finance

Bank. For example, in 2008 when the Masomo Education Foundation found itself unable to support a third scholarship, it was Finance Bank that stepped in to provide funds for the third student.

Despite this, few politicians would want to publicise their association with Mahtani. And yet Michael Sata (both as opposition leader and as president) chose this man to be a confidant. Sata certainly had a sense of loyalty and a sense of self-preservation which may explain his relationships with the likes of Kenneth Kaunda, Xavier Chungu and Lombe Chibesakunda. His relationship with Mahtani however revealed extreme loyalty bordering on defiance. I have seen a letter from Michael Sata to Rajan Mahtani which starts with the salutation, 'My dear Rajan.'' There can be little doubt Rajan Lekhraj Mahtani put letters like this to good business use.

CHAPTER TEN

Not so Allergic to Corruption

Michael Sata was not an overly greedy man. At the time of his election as president he lived in a comfortable but not opulent home situated at 3 Omelo Mumba Road in Lusaka's Rhodes Park district. The outward wealth enjoyed by Sata was consistent with his work history. Unlike so many other politicians of his generation, Sata had not come into sudden wealth after Zambia attained her independence. Sata had a well-documented career path.

After a one year stint at Katibunga Seminary, Sata moved to another catechist school in Isoka district called Kantensha. He spent three years at this school before leaving in 1951. That year Sata took advantage of the fact that some missionary schools had established secondary school courses by correspondence. One such school was Lubushi Seminary near Kasama where, in addition to clergy training, Sata received the junior high school certificate after successfully completing his long distance studies.

Possessing a junior secondary school certificate placed Sata amongst the most educated black Northern Rhodesians in 1956. This was to prove advantageous as Sata left rural Mpika for the rapidly urbanising Copperbelt in 1957.

Once on the Copperbelt, the future president joined the Northern Rhodesia Police. According to the US based Zambian media practitioner, Field Ruwe, Sata's timing could not have been better as Police Commissioner Colonel John Patrick Fforde was then looking for 'native' police officers to beef up his colonial force. Of the 1,720 natives recruited, only a handful could match Sata's academic qualifications. Sata was therefore a highly prized recruit.

He did not however last long in the police service as by 1959 he was imprisoned for inciting violence and sentenced to two years in prison. It appears he was released from prison after 16 months.

By 1961 he had joined a large construction company called Roberts Construction (Central Africa) Limited. Sata was 24 at the time but his young age did not prevent him from becoming general secretary of the National Union of Engineering, Construction and General Workers. He maintained his interest in trade union activities until 1964 when he went into private business and opened an industrial relations firm. Two years later he had become an associate of the Institute of Personnel Managers as well as a founder member of the Zambia Institute of Human Resource Management.

Furthermore, Sata sat on the board of Trans-Africa Safaris Limited, an established South African company specialising in taxidermy—the art of preparing, stuffing, and mounting the skins of animals. Sata's association with Trans-Africa Safaris brought him in contact with many influential business people both at home and abroad.

These connections were important as the young budding businessman contemplated his future. He left Zambia for the United Kingdom in 1970 with a view to furthering his education. It is not clear however what Sata studied while in England but it is understood that in addition to his studies he also worked for a living. Ruwe has suggested that the future president "worked at Victoria Station and other [stations] around the country" as a shunter, conductor, and locomotive driver. (*Michael Chilufya Sata Biography, Lusaka Times*, February 03, 2014.) If Ruwe is correct, the view reported by most British newspapers when Sata won the presidency that the new leader had been a porter at Victoria Station, may be simplistic and unduly dismissive.

Sata returned to Zambia armed with a huge amount of experience that was to serve him well as a businessman. Among other accomplishments he was managing director of Tanners and Taxidermists (Zambia), executive chairman of the Ndola Inn Limited, director of Delta Electrical Contractors, and project director of the extremely lucrative Avondale Housing Estates Limited.

Most of Sata's history after this period is well known. The point of the background above is to show that Sata had had ample opportunity to earn an honest living and lawfully build significant personal assets. He did not have to resort to corruption to do that.

Thus when President Michael Sata said on October 14, 2011 that he wanted to draft a new constitution by the end of the year as part of his drive to weed out corruption and change the way Zambia did business, he sounded credible to those who knew him.

"We attach great importance to issue of good governance," he emphasised.

Indeed Sata did subsequently honour his commitment to strengthen anti-corruption legislation by putting back on the statute books the offence of abuse of office, which the previous government had repealed. His government did also "investigate acts of corruption by the previous government," as promised in the first speech to parliament. Sata summarised his reaction to the scourge of corruption in this memorable phrase: 'I'm allergic to corruption'

One of his first acts as president was to dismiss the head of the Anti-Corruption Commission, Godfrey Kayukwa, who had been accused of bungling graft investigations and was seen by Transparency International Zambia and opposition leaders as being unduly close to the outgoing head of state Rupiah Banda. Both TIZ and the opposition leaders had called for Kayukwa's resignation.

Sata was also irked by the Banda government's refusal to appeal the corruption acquittal of former president Frederick Chiluba, a former ally and now political foe of Sata.

But Banda's prosecutors may have been right when they decided not to appeal the acquittal. The Chiluba case attracted much commentary but few of the commentators stopped to examine the evidence. The case of theft of $480,000 by President Chiluba over a ten year period was based on the fact that that amount of money had been drawn out of the Zambia Security Intelligence Service account known as Zamtrop.

The other side of the coin however is that rather more than the amount alleged to have been stolen had been deposited into the Zamtrop account by Chiluba on the advice of the director general of intelligence. Chiluba was the recipient of huge amounts of money from the Libyan leader Colonel Muammar Qaddafi in appreciation of his efforts to have Qaddafi elected as the first chair of the African Union. Chiluba had also received monies from Jose Eduardo dos Santos, the Angolan leader for his role in ending the civil war in the former Portuguese colony. When I spoke to Chiluba at his residence in Lusaka in 2008 he did not deny receipt of payments from these two leaders. Indeed the Chiluba defence team argued during the corruption trial in Zambia that more than $8.5m of cash payments to the president had gone through the Zamtrop account, and that these monies were for Mr Chiluba to spend as he wished.

These monies were deposited into the Zamtrop account on the advice of Xavier Chungu the then director general of ZSIS. Evidence given by Chungu's successor as director general was that the management of the Zamtrop account was "entirely under the Director General who is the controlling officer." The magistrate found that as a matter of law the Director-General was not obliged to disclose the source of the money or its purpose.

Lusaka magistrate Jones Chinyama therefore found that the prosecution team had failed to prove the case against Chiluba. Given the categorical nature of the law and the clear evidence showing that the money used by Chiluba had been deposited into the account from non-Zambian government sources, it may well have been futile to appeal this decision.

Be that as it may, it was encouraging that Sata, a largely self-made businessman, was keen to fight corruption and was making unequivocal statements in that regard, and indeed occasionally taking action to stamp out the scourge.

Sadly, Sata's health was rapidly deteriorating making it impossible for him to provide more than anaemic leadership. While the Sata regime was able to prosecute a few individuals, the administration appears to have made no impact with respect to combating systemic or institutional corruption.

Systemic corruption could not be addressed in the absence of a president firmly in control of his party and the government. Within two years of winning the election it became clear to alert observers that the PF had split into two main factions. One of the factions was clearly led by Wynter Kabimba, the party secretary general who also served as Minister of Justice. Kabimba was also increasingly beginning to see himself as Co-President. The leadership of the other faction did not rest in one individual but was supported (at least in subterranean fashion) by the Finance Minister, Alexander Bwalya Chikwanda as well as Godfrey Bwalya Mwamba, the Defence Minister.

Until mid-2013, the Kabimba faction appeared to be in the ascendency. Kabimba had called for President Sata to be declared without opposition as the PF candidate in the 2016 presidential election. Kabimba must have known that the president's health was such that he was unlikely to be alive in 2016 and if he was he would be in no state to run for anything, least of all the Zambian presidency. Kabimba's move was therefore seen as a false declaration of loyalty designed to give him an advantage in the fight to replace Sata as president.

It did not take long for accusations of disloyalty to surface. On September 03, 2013, Charles Sakala of *Zambia Reports* informed his readers that the PF Southern Province deputy information and publicity secretary Brighton Luhyila had declared his province a no-go area for Mr. Kabimba. Luhyila was blunt in his view of Kabimba. He called the secretary general "a traitor" as he accused him of plotting a palace coup against President Sata.

In a sign that Kabimba may not have had as much control over the PF cadres as he often suggested, Luhyila had prior to his anti Kabimba declaration led scores of placard waving party members along the main thoroughfare of Livingstone to show support for Sata's candidature in 2016.

The old Sata would have ended the infighting quickly and reasserted his authority. He would have also understood that discontent against his secretary general was real. But the ailing president let the wrangles go on for almost a year after Luhyila had declared the PF secretary general unwelcome in the Southern Province.

Wynter Kabimba was finally dismissed on August 28, 2014.

Defence Minister Edgar Lungu, a member of the anti Kabimba faction, was appointed Secretary- General. Not only did Mr. Lungu keep his defence portfolio, he also assumed additional responsibilities as Justice Minister. This was a clear sign from Sata that Lungu was the heir apparent.

Since Kabimba was an appointed (as opposed to elected) Member of Parliament, he also lost his seat in parliament.

The development was seen as a huge victory for the Finance Minister Alexander Chikwanda, who had been targeted in a corruption scandal that was allegedly leaked by the Kabimba faction to the press. It would now perhaps be only a matter of time before Mutembo Nchito, the tainted director of public prosecutions who had reportedly been preparing a case against Chikwanda, was dealt with. The other member of the alleged pro Kabimba 'cartel' Fred M'membe would be harder to deal with since he published his own newspaper. But even for him it would only be a matter of time before there was a noticeable decline in his influence.

Why Fight Corruption?

The internal squabbles in the PF culminating in the dismissal of Kabimba and (later) the dismissal of the director of public prosecutions distracted the nation from the issue of fighting both petty and systematic or structural corruption. The UNIP era idea that corruption was whatever the ruler of the day deemed it to be was reinforced by PF infighting. The UNIP approach allowed corrupt officials favoured by the authorities to escape punishment, even in the face of overwhelming evidence. On the other hand persons disliked by the regime would be hounded for corrupt practices, however thin the evidence against them.

The case of Henry Shamabanse is an example of a favoured politician being shielded from punishment even in the face of overwhelming evidence of wrongdoing.

Henry Shamabanse was a Minister of State for the Central Province in the mid-1960s. He was then appointed to the corresponding position in the Southern Province and by virtue of that position became the chair of the Southern Province African Farming Improvement Fund or SPAFIF as it was commonly known. SPAFIF was controlled by a board of directors consisting of Mr Shamabanse, as chair, and other members appointed by him from time to time.

The purpose of SPAFIF was to promote better farming methods among African farmers in the Southern Province. This was typically done by the provision of loans for the execution of eligible projects. For example, SPAFIF would provide finance for projects such as dams, roads, storm drains and other works beneficial to area farmers. At one point SPAFIF had a policy to lend only to groups of farmers rather than individuals. That was certainly the case in June 1968. Five months later the policy changed and SPAFIF was allowed to once again lend to individual farmers.

Mr Shamabanse owned a farm in the Central Province which he wanted to improve. In November 1968 when the SPAFIF board was once again able to lend to individuals, Mr Shamabanse sought money for the development of his own farm. He decided to do so by obtaining two loans in the amount of Zambian Kwacha 7,500 (about US$8,000 at the time) in the name of a man called Benkele. This was in violation of the African Farming Improvement Funds Act which restricted the granting of loans "to farmers in the area for which the Board has been established"; in this case the Southern Province. Mr Shamabanse had also obtained a loan of US$5,500 through the agency of an intermediary company at a time when the board policy was not to lend to individuals.

He was charged on three counts of corruption in respect of the three loans and convicted in the magistrate's court on all counts. He appealed to the High Court where all three convictions were quashed. Unhappy with the High Court's decision, the director of public prosecutions appealed to the Supreme Court. The Supreme Court acquitted Mr Shamabanse on a technicality with respect to the counts relating to the loans amounting to $8,000, but convicted him on the count relating to the $5,500 loan. Shamabanse was sentenced to eight months imprisonment with hard labour.

The Shamabanse case was one of the earliest cases of corruption in Zambia, and how this politician was treated was to influence the fight against corruption in future years. Mr Shamabanse never served his prison term because within days President Kaunda pardoned him. The president went further and reappointed him Minister of State, this time in the North Western Province.

The clear message from Kaunda was that different rules would apply for those with connections to the ruling elite. The president's action did nothing to discourage corruption. It did however assure potentially and actually corrupt leaders that in times of difficulty they could count on the president for help, as long as they were loyal to Kaunda and his political party. Once again it paid to belong to UNIP.

Subsequent regimes have similarly rewarded loyal party officials although the more transparent system they have operated in has not given them the same freedom that Kaunda had.

In its most basic form, corruption is the misuse of public power for private gain. The misuse is typically authored by an elected official or public servant. This basic definition would be consistent with the understanding of the majority of Zambians who abhor corruption. It is for this reason that there was such an outcry in the country when the MMD government decriminalised the offence of abuse of office during the Rupiah Banda presidency. Sata rightly won praise when he reinstated the offence.

Even so, the basic definition lacks the comprehensiveness and precision of science. So let's try a definition from Petrus van Duyne, emeritus professor at Tilburg University in the Netherlands. He defines corruption as:

> an improbity or decay in the decision-making process in which a decision-maker consents to deviate or demands deviation from the criterion which should rule his or her decision-making, in exchange for a reward or for the promise or expectation of a reward, while these motives influencing his or her decision-making cannot be part of the justification of the decision.

This definition envisages an official using the decision making process for personal gain. The definition would cover both petty and systemic corruption. Petty corruption might, for example, involve a police officer at a road block declining to charge a motorist with defective lights with an offence in return for a payment by the motorist to the officer in her personal capacity.

Systemic corruption would be corruption occurring primarily as a result of weaknesses of an organization or process. Thus the payment in the above example could result from systemic failures such as lack of adequate supervision and insufficient remuneration of police officers.

Systemic corruption creates opportunities for routine graft. Consider the effect of President Sata's keenness to expand Zambia's infrastructure and his decision to embark on an ambitious road construction programme called Link Zambia 8000 whose aim was to construct or rehabilitate an 8000 kilometre road network.

It did not take long for allegations of corruption to emerge in the awarding of contracts. The president's own involvement in the award of the contracts on the pretext that the head of state had power to provide additional supervision to that of the Road Development Agency did not help. At a cost of $1 million per kilometre for a possible eventual outlay of $8 billion, there was great potential for major corruption involving large payments and many beneficiaries.

But the ambitious road development plan also provided President Sata an opportunity to fight systemic corruption by insisting on proper tender procedures accompanied by robust and transparent supervision of the entire process. Sadly he was too unwell to effectively supervise the existing system let alone improve on it. The warring factions within his administration took advantage of this and extorted money from contractors in the president's name. I spoke to a foreign born contractor who told me that he had personally paid "hundreds of thousands of dollars" in bribes in order to get contracts that he felt he would have won anyway under a fair tender system. These payments were over and above amounts paid to politicians during election campaigns. In this regard he pegged his contribution at $ 20,000.

The contractor also extravagantly claimed that Michael Sata himself had pocketed "a billion dollars" whose transfer from the country had been facilitated by Rajan Mahtani, the controversial businessman. I do not doubt that this contractor paid huge amounts of money to corrupt Zambian officials in order to obtain road construction contracts. I have heard similar accounts from other business people. I do not doubt either that the Zambian business community, particularly the Indo-Zambian community, is placed under tremendous pressure during election campaigns to contribute to the governing party and to credible opposition parties. That is also supported by other independent evidence.

What I do question is the claim that Sata himself took bribes amounting to a billion dollars and externalised this amount through Mahtani's bank.

There are three reasons for my disbelief. The first is that for the greater part of his presidency, Sata was not sufficiently fit, mentally or physically, to arrange such an elaborate scheme. The second is that after his death, his estate was not unusually large, with most of the assets like real estate having been acquired before Sata became president. The third reason is that at the time of Sata's death the best estimate was that 1900 kilometres had been rehabilitated or built under the Link Zambia 8000 road construction programme. In the words of Yamfwa Mukanga, the Minister of Transport, Works, Supply and Communications:

> We have engaged a number of contractors to carry out rehabilitation and upgrading works on our road networks, so far 1,900 kilometres of roads out of the 8,000 have been worked on with a total cost of K7.1 billion.

The minister was responding to allegations by the Member of Parliament for Lubansenshi constituency that corruption had "been taken to State House in the supervision of RDA."

The minister's intent in giving these figures was to demonstrate how hard the government was working. We can therefore assume that the amount of work done did not exceed 1900 kilometres. If it had, the minister would only have been too keen to claim the credit. We should also bear in mind that the 1900 kilometres did not represent new roads but also included roads that were being rehabilitated rather than built from scratch. The cost of these roads would of course be substantially less than the estimated $1 million per kilometre. Since close to half the work done would have been on existing roads, the amount spent by the government on the

1900 kilometres would have been about $1 billion, roughly K7.1 billion, as indicated by the minister. It simply does not make sense that all of this money would have gone into the president's pocket, and the builders of the roads would have been paid nothing!

Incidentally, it took another 20 months after Sata's death before the government reached 3, 947 km of roads under Link Zambia 8000. (*Lusaka Times May 13, 2016*) Sata would have been proud to hear his protégé and successor, Edgar Lungu announce at a press conference as the Zambian winter was dawning that more than $93 million had been collected from newly established toll gates.

Nonetheless President Sata did miss the opportunity to end systemic corruption in road construction. Corruption may not have disappeared completely from Zambian society during his stay in office but it would have been significantly reduced, to the benefit of the poor and vulnerable who had worked so hard to put Mr. Sata in State House. It goes without saying that all corruption costs are paid by the consumer and the tax-payer. Zambian consumers and tax payers have continued to pay that cost as systemic corruption in road construction has continued unabated.

In March 2015, the National Road Fund Agency announced the 2015 road sector budget. It was worth K5.4 billion ($692 million), representing 11% of the K46.7 billion ($5.9 billion) National Budget. The Road Development Agency received K4.9 billion ($628 million). The Ministry of Local Government and Housing received K259 million ($ 33.2 million). The other significant beneficiary in the sector, the Road Transport and Safety Agency got K205 million ($26 million.)

Critics of the PF government continued with the criticism they had first levelled at Sata when he showed enthusiasm for expanding the national infrastructure. They charged that Sata was misguided because there were more pressing challenges such as hunger. 'People cannot eat roads,' was a popular slogan in opposition circles.

Sata was in fact right to pay attention to infrastructure development and the road sector budget announced five months after his death was consistent with the World Bank's recommendation that 10-20% of developing countries' budgets should go towards transport sector infrastructure. The reason for this is that an extensive and well-maintained network of primary, secondary, and feeder roads is critical for economic growth and poverty alleviation. There is no shortage of evidence to show that investment in roads boosts agricultural productivity and growth.

I pointed out for example in *Getting Zambia to Work* that in times of drought the southern part of Zambia experiences food shortages even as the Luapula province enjoys surpluses of food that cannot be transported to southern markets for want of a good road network. The conclusion reached by the World Bank is that adequate and continuous investment in roads leads to positive growth in labour productivity. It follows that well planned, routinely maintained, and safe roads are critical for economic growth and poverty alleviation.

The issue then is not that Mr. Sata and his government paid too much attention to road infrastructure. Rather the issue is that having embarked on an ambitious plan to improve Zambia's infrastructure, nothing was done to address corruption in the road sector.

The World Bank estimates that global corruption in transport projects account for anywhere between 5% and 20% of transaction costs. Given China's status as a major player in road construction in Zambia it is noteworthy that companies from China, which according to the country's Vice Commerce

Minister, Zhong Shan, invested $102.9 billion abroad in 2014, are seen as the most likely to pay bribes abroad. The other country in this league of corruption is Russia.

With respect to sector corruption, the Organization for Economic Co-operation and Development analysed 427 cases of bribery in international business in 2014. Two-thirds of the cases occurred in just four industries: extractive (19%); construction (15%); transportation and storage (15%); and information and communication (10%).

Senior executives were involved in more than half the cases, with chief executive officers playing an active role in 12%. The OECD found that in these instances the CEOs either paid the bribes themselves, or authorized them.

Civil servants and employees of state-owned companies were most likely to be the target of foreign corruption. They were promised, offered or given bribes in 80% of the cases. These included top politicians, such as government ministers, and heads of state companies. Officials working in customs, health and defence were also likely to be recipients.

There is a pecking order in dishing out dirty money. The higher ranking the official, the bigger the bribe. While heads of states and ministers were bribed in only 5% of the cases, they received 11% of total bribes. Customs officials on the other hand, were targeted in 11% of cases, but pocketed little more than 1% of the bribes.

So, we have a major player in Zambian construction with a reputation for corruption and a sector with a reputation for extreme corruption. That deadly combination cries out for reform.

A Missed Opportunity to Fight Corruption

President Sata was in many ways uniquely placed to successfully combat corruption in Zambia. The scourge could have been addressed by turning incentives to be corrupt into punishments; strengthening the public service by making it more independent and professional in addition to strengthening existing institutions designed to combat corruption; and galvanising opposition to corruption.

Rwanda under Paul Kagame is a good example of how corruption can be successfully fought. Sata would have done well to emulate Rwanda's example. It is no accident that the African Union's Advisory Board on Corruption and the UN Economic Commission for Africa (UNECA) chose Rwanda as the venue for Africa's Anti-Corruption Week in December 2012.

Kagame understood that corruption could not be defeated without turning incentives for corruption into punishments. In Zambia many corrupt public officials rely on the assumption that as long as they are loyal to the president and his administration, they will be reasonably safe from scrutiny and punishment. The absence of strong institutions to monitor and punish corruption is also an incentive to be corrupt.

In contrast, it is mandatory in Kagame's Rwanda for all high-level officials, including the President, cabinet Ministers, and Directors-Generals (Permanent Secretaries), to declare their assets before, during, and after, leaving office. These declarations are not done simply for the purpose of ticking a box on a check list but are used as a tool to investigate the origins of the assets to make sure that what has been declared on paper matches the actual wealth of declarants.

Rwanda's Leadership Code of Conduct for public officials requires affected officials to submit this information every 30th of June, to the Office of the Ombudsman. Failure to meet the deadline leads to sanctions such as a warning, suspension, 25% cut in salary, dismissal, public censure, and prosecution, depending on the circumstances. There was some resistance to comply with the Code of Conduct when the anti-corruption campaign started in 2004, but this quickly changed when officials realised that severe punishments would be meted out regardless of the rank or influence of the offender. Asset declaration forms are kept confidential, but the Ombudsman's office does routine on the ground investigations for the purpose of confirming what has been declared by the officials.

Zambia too has an Ombudsman that could be used in the same way as her Rwandan counterpart. But in the absence of political leadership committed to transparency the office of the Zambian Ombudsman is all but invisible as Edgar Lungu observed in September 2014 while serving as Minister of Justice. More seriously, the Zambian Ombudsman is hopelessly under resourced.

In June 2008 Investigator General (Ombudsman) Caroline Sokoni revealed that her office only had two investigators. For this reason, the Ombudsman was being hampered in her efforts to carry out her constitutional duties. The situation was not too different in 2015 when the Office of the Investigator General was largely inactive. That is a pity because this is an important office in the fight against corruption and the promotion of good governance.

Since the constitutional mandate of the Ombudsman is to oversee government administration and to check the abuses of power by public officials, we can assume that given the challenges described above, there is in fact no institution in Zambia today that has responsibility for this mandate. It is worth recalling the reason for the introduction of this office in Zambia in 1972. At that time cases of corruption and abuse of power were becoming rampant and the concern was that without an Ombudsman, the situation would get completely out of hand and erode the very fabric of Zambian society.

The effect of underfunding the Office of the Ombudsman is that many corrupt officials escape censure. When she addressed the National Constitutional Conference public service committee in June 2008, Ms. Sokoni said her office received one million complaints a year but she could only attend to a fraction of these complaints because of her office's resource limitations.

Ms Sokoni would have been justified in calling for a strengthening of her office by making it more independent. Under the law in effect until 2016, the Investigator General reported directly to the Republican President who was also her appointing authority. Given the president's power and the demands on the office, this arrangement was clearly unhelpful in efforts to promote good governance. Any president is potentially an abuser of power just by virtue of having so much of it. Also, the president is too busy to get meaningful reports and take action on the one million complaints that the Ombudsman receives each year.

An obvious reform here would be to change the reporting relationship and make the Ombudsman accountable to the people of Zambia through parliament.

This is precisely what happened on 5 January 2016 when President Edgar Lungu signed Constitution Bill Number 17 of 2015 which converted the Office of the Investigator General into the Office of the Public Protector.

This constitutional innovation represents more than a name change, providing the institution of the public protector the power and authority to function as a Parliamentary Ombudsman.

Although the constitutional amendment provides for the appointment of a public protector by the president on the recommendation of the Judicial Service Commission, subject to ratification by the National Assembly, the public protector who has powers equivalent to a High Court Judge, reports, not to the president but to the National Assembly. Thus the public protector is not answerable to the president.

While the office of the investigator general merely made recommendations to the institutions complained against, the new office of public protector has real powers and can, among other things:

Investigate an action or decision taken or omitted to be taken by a state institution in the performance of an administrative function.

Bring an action before a court of law.

Hear an appeal by a person relating to an action or decision taken or omitted to be taken in respect of that person.

Make a decision on an action to be taken against a public officer or constitutional office holder, which decision must then be implemented by an appropriate authority.

The importance of this reform may best be illustrated by the following question: Under the pre 2016 law, could the president be compelled to take action in response to allegations of abuse of power by the president himself?

In answering this question we must remember that the complaints made to the ombudsman were examined in confidence, and the public only became aware of those complaints that were eventually fully investigated and reported.

President Sata missed the opportunity to galvanise public opinion in the fight against corruption. The old Sata was particularly gifted at communicating with what politicians refer to as 'ordinary Zambians'. Sadly the new Sata's talent in this area was discreet. Perhaps he would have performed better had he been in good health. The effect of this would have been to catalyse forces of change keen to end corruption. These forces would have gained invaluable credibility by having the president as their champion. In these circumstances, the work done by the ombudsman would have acquired a new urgency, leading to appropriate funding levels.

This is in effect what President Kagame did. His government took the fight against corruption to the people and made it their fight. All districts in the country were encouraged to get involved and meaningful but inexpensive incentives were put in place to encourage citizen participation in the good fight. Thus an annual competition and awards system was instituted. Districts obtaining high marks for their anti-corruption and good governance work were recognised nationally by way of trophies and certificates.

To ensure that the principles of transparency and good governance were inculcated into the national culture, the anti-corruption campaign focused on the youth as future leaders. Anti-corruption awareness campaigns in high schools and tertiary institutions continue to be a feature of life for young Rwandese.

These efforts have paid off as evidenced by the number of international companies willing to invest in Rwanda and citing the relative absence of corruption there as a major reason for choosing that destination. This was not the case in 2004 when the impressive journey to transparency began.

In 2008 Rwanda placed 102 out of 175 countries on Transparency International's Perception Index. In other words only 73 other countries had a worse reputation for corruption. Five years after commencement of the anti-corruption campaign, Rwanda went to 89th place. In 2010 it took the 66th position. In 2014 Rwanda was at number 55, ahead of such countries as Croatia, Ghana, Greece, Macedonia, South Africa, and Turkey. In 2015 Rwanda moved up to number 44 ahead of Georgia, Namibia, Mauritius, and Jordan. Zambia was at number 76, the same ranking as Bosnia i Herzegovina, Brazil, and India.

President Sata would have done well to pay attention to the fight against corruption in Rwanda. Had he done that, he would have understood that it was not enough to simply declare an allergy to corruption. The lesson from Rwanda is that leadership and political will are indispensable in the fight against this insidious scourge. Good leadership recognises the importance of strengthening public institutions, galvanising citizens and making them proud warriors in the fight against corruption.

Easy Targets

Failure to tackle institutional or structural corruption did not mean total abandonment of the fight against corruption. The Sata government, like its predecessors, used anti-corruption legislation to pursue easy targets like political opponents, and others whose prosecution would have no negative effect on the regime. This is not to suggest that evidence was fabricated against these people but rather to assert that there were other alleged offenders in similar circumstances who escaped prosecution simply because they were favoured by the regime, as Henry Shamabanse had been favoured by the Kaunda regime. The difference this time was that the government had more influence over a less independent prosecution service.

On January 30, 2014 Levy Mwanawasa's former private secretary, Moses Muteteka was jailed for five years after being convicted of the offence of theft of motor vehicle. It was alleged that Muteteka, on May 24, 2010 while in Lusaka, stole a Mitsubishi Fuso light truck which was rightfully the property of Chibombo District Council whose geographic area coincided with Muteteka's own parliamentary constituency. The fact that Muteteka caused this vehicle to be registered in his name was used by the convicting magistrate as proof of the theft.

The proceedings themselves appear to have been conducted in accordance with established Zambian and international standards of adjudication.

Even so, members of the public were concerned that Muteteka should be only one of a handful of public officials to be convicted for a practice that is not uncommon in Zambia. The universality of this practice was hinted at by the anti-corruption watchdog Transparency International Zambia whose executive director, Goodwell Lungu, welcomed the conviction but warned that there were other leaders who also deserved punishment. Lungu took the opportunity to advise these leaders to learn a lesson from Muteteka's conviction.

Another easy target in the fight against corruption was Andrew Banda, President Rupiah Banda's likable but mischievous son.

Andrew Banda served as third secretary at the Zambian High Commission in Ottawa in the early 1990s. His tenure came to an abrupt end after he used his official position to obtain an air ticket from Fairlawn Travel; a Nepean based travel agency, to travel to Zambia on personal business. The country was caused much embarrassment when Fairlawn Travel went public and complained that the Zambian government had failed to pay for the ticket. A reporter for *the Ottawa Citizen* went so far as to suggest sarcastically that the next time Canada sent aid money to Zambia it should deduct the amount the Zambian High Commission owed Fairlawn Travel. The Zambian mission on the other hand took the position that the travel agency should have been more diligent in determining whether Banda was indeed travelling on official business. Steve Buck, the Fairlawn executive responsible for the account, countered that the agency had in fact placed a call to the mission and an officer there had confirmed that Banda was indeed travelling on official business. Steve Buck was not to know that the 'officer' at the mission was in fact a Banda plant.

On his return from Zambia, Banda was immediately placed on mandatory leave of absence and the High Commissioner, Joshua Siyolwe, instituted an investigation into the matter. The investigation found that Banda had behaved inappropriately, and he was dismissed from diplomatic service. No criminal charges were laid against Banda on that occasion.

He was not so lucky in 2014.

On Friday September 14 of that year, Andrew Banda was sentenced to two years imprisonment with hard labour for soliciting a two per cent cut on all contracts awarded by the Road Development Agency (RDA) to the Italian construction company Fratelli Locci.

After almost a decade in the political wilderness, Banda was rehabilitated by his father Rupiah who had now taken over the presidency following the death of President Mwanawasa. Rupiah Banda decided to send his son to Italy as Zambia's first secretary at the embassy in Rome.

The state's central allegation in the corruption case against the 53 year old Banda was that between September 1, 2010 and December 31, 2011, as first secretary at the Zambian Embassy in Italy and later as Deputy High Commissioner to India, he solicited and received two per cent gratification on all payments made to Fratelli Locci SRI Limited by the Road Development Agency.

The magistrate had no difficulty in finding Banda guilty. The conviction however only served to remind the public about the pervasive nature of corruption and the selectiveness of prosecutions. Responding to the conviction, Elias Chipimo the leader of the National Restoration Party (NAREP) expressed concern about the frequency of kickbacks "within the country's governance structure."

Chipimo also expressed concern that the fight against corruption was not prosecuted with equal vigour when the culprits were connected to the leadership of the country. In his words:

> It is very important that this fight we are being told the PF is purportedly waging against corruption is not seen to be a selective exercise. We see where people are connected to the ruling administration the fight against corruption doesn't seem to be proceeding with a similar amount of vigour.

Less clear cut was the case against former president Rupiah Banda. Mr. Banda was accused of concluding a government-to-government oil contract between Zambia and Nigeria when he was in office between 2008 and 2011 with a view to benefiting himself and his family to the tune of $2.5 million.

I had great difficulty following this case when it was reported in the newspapers. On many occasions I wondered why the prosecution had been commenced at all. It simply was never explained how Banda benefited from the contract.

Joshua Banda, the same magistrate who had convicted Andrew Banda clearly had similar challenges. On June 29, 2015 he acquitted the former president on the basis that "There [was] no evidence tendered regarding the proof of the transfer of the money and that Banda and his family benefited [from the alleged transaction]."

The magistrate found the evidence before the court insufficient to warrant a conviction. He applied a common sense approach in reaching the conclusion that there was insufficient evidence to warrant conviction. He asked why in a contract of this nature no official from Nigeria had been called to testify.

It was a reasonable question. Why did no one in the government make arrangements for key witnesses from Nigeria to testify? Could it be there were no such witnesses and Rupiah Banda's prosecution was simply a form of harassment? Given the thinness of the legal basis for commencing the prosecution, many Banda supporters answered the question in the affirmative.

President Rupiah Banda should never have been prosecuted. He was guaranteed immunity from prosecution by the country's constitution as a former head of state. Because of a rash need to punish for acts of corruption and abuse of office that allegedly took place during Banda's rule, state agents moved speedily and thoughtlessly to persuade parliament to remove Banda's immunity from prosecution. It transpired later that the resolution by the National Assembly to strip the former president of his immunity in March 2013 may itself have been unconstitutional in that it did not specify the reasons for such a move. When Banda challenged the removal of his immunity in the High Court it soon became clear that the state had indeed acted rashly. In order to avoid embarrassment, the state quickly agreed with Banda's lawyers on March 16, 2016 to a consent judgment, allowing the court to quash the decision by the Director of Public Prosecutions to prosecute Mr Banda for abuse of authority and other corrupt practices. Mr. Banda's immunity from prosecution was thus restored.

The Danger of Selective Prosecution

Targeted prosecutions like the ones above are more likely to happen in jurisdictions where the prosecution agencies and even the judiciary are compromised. Prosecution agencies that lack independence and professionalism will sooner or later find themselves being used by political masters to suppress or harass legitimate political opposition.

Michael Sata had seen the danger of this when he was an opposition leader. Sadly, he did nothing to fortify the independence of the judiciary and prosecution agencies after he got into office. Sata should have moved quickly to strengthen the independence of both the judiciary and the prosecutorial arms of government. He would have been on solid constitutional ground had he, for example, insisted on real independence for the National Prosecution Authority.

Article 180 (1) of the new Zambian Constitution follows article 216(1) of the old one by creating the position of a Director of Public Prosecutions appointed by the Republican President, subject to ratification by the National Assembly. By law the person appointed as director of prosecutions must have experience in undertaking criminal trials, and must also be eligible for appointment as a high court judge.

The Director of Public Prosecutions is recognised by the constitution as the chief prosecutor for the Government. In addition, he or she also becomes the head of the National Prosecutions Authority.

The Director of Public Prosecutions is given wide ranging powers with respect to the commencement of prosecutions and their discontinuance prior to judgment. In keeping with the broad powers conferred on the office, the Director of Public Prosecutions (DPP) cannot be subjected to the direction or control of a person or an authority in the performance of the functions of her office. The DPP is however required to have regard to the public interest, administration of justice, the integrity of the judicial system and the need to prevent and avoid abuse of the legal process in the exercise of her functions.

The constitution therefore appears to confer supremacy on the DPP in matters of prosecution. It does not limit the DPP with respect to the kinds of crimes she can prosecute. This creates potential tension with the Anti-Corruption Commission (ACC) which sees itself as the lead institution in the fight against corruption in Zambia. The Commission's promotional literature says in addition to establishing corruption prevention mechanisms, the ACC has a duty to investigate cases of corruption and prosecute suspected offenders.

What would happen if there were a conflict between the Director of Public Prosecutions and the Anti-Corruption Commission? Supposing the ACC declined to cooperate with the Director of Public Prosecutions with respect to a particular matter, would the DPP, as chief prosecutor for the government direct the Anti-Corruption Commission to do the needful? Not according to Section 5 of the 1996 *Anti-Corruption Commission Act* which states that the Commission *"shall not, in the performance of its duties, be subject to the direction or control of any person or authority."*

The Virtue of Impartial Prosecution

Elevating the profile of the National Prosecution Authority would encourage the perception that the prosecution process in Zambia is impartial, as public attention will probably shift from an individual office holder (the Director of Public Prosecutions) to an institution.

In this new world the National Prosecution Authority (NPA) would be categorical about its mandate and values. First and foremost the public would need to be assured that strengthening the NPA was a deliberate act aimed at making transparent the principle of prosecutorial independence, free from any improper influence, including executive influence.

The NPA must be driven by a mission to serve the public by prosecuting cases with diligence, in a manner that is not selective but is fair, impartial and objective. In prosecuting matters the NPA must see itself not only as upholder of the law but also as visible protector of the rights of individuals.

Ideally the NPA should report to Parliament through either the Attorney General or the Director of Public Prosecutions. Even so, there should be a healthy distance between the NPA and the Attorney General or Director of Public Prosecutions as the case may be. In the past, some Attorneys-Generals have allowed themselves to be used by the executive branch for purposes of improperly influencing prosecutors.

There will always be a need for consultation between the Attorney General and the Director of Public Prosecutions on matters of import to society, but this relationship must be premised on the principles of respect for the independence of the prosecution function.

In order to ensure that such consultations are conducted properly there should be a requirement that all instructions from the Attorney General be in writing and published in the Government Gazette. This may appear unduly onerous to some but this is doable and worth the effort. The Public Prosecution Service of Canada, for example, has such an arrangement between itself and the Canadian Attorney General.

In the Canadian model there is a reciprocal requirement that the Director of Public Prosecutions informs the Attorney

General of any prosecution or planned intervention that may raise important questions of general interest, allowing the Attorney General the opportunity to intervene in, or assume conduct of, a case. Additionally, the PPSC must provide the Attorney General with an annual report for tabling in Parliament.

There has been concern over the past few years that the Zambian judicial system may actually be compromised. This has been a result of perception that some magistrates and even judges have allowed themselves to be improperly influenced by litigants. The second reason is that prosecutors have not been seen to be fulfilling their ethical, procedural, and constitutional obligations. The zeal showed in the prosecution of political opponents has convinced many Zambians that prosecutors are more like partisan advocates than representatives of justice. A well-functioning National Prosecutions Authority with an appropriate mandate supported by suitable values can convince the Zambian public that the purpose of a criminal prosecution is not so much to obtain a conviction, as it is to lay before the court what the State considers to be credible evidence pertinent to the alleged crime.

When that happens, Zambians will once again have full confidence in their prosecutorial agencies.

The Danger of Institutionalised Corruption in the Judicial Sector

Until Zambia has a judicial and prosecutorial system that is transparent and strictly rules based, there will be the danger not only of individual victimisation by the law but also group victimisation.

The controversial American author and journalist, Dr Les Sachs has highlighted the dangers of corruption in the US legal system. Although Dr Sachs is often accused of going 'over the top,' his basic points when they are backed by facts serve as a good lesson for a young country like Zambia.

Sachs believes that the American judicial system is the most corrupt in the world. One of the reasons for this is that the US system targets minorities and low income people for persecution by way of imprisonment. There is a history behind this that Zambia should note. While most Americans deeply believe in democracy and fair play, there are many powerful citizens who appear to believe that some Americans are less worthy than others. These 'lesser' Americans are targeted for over policing and prosecution.

The end result is that the United States has two million prisoners or 25 per cent of the entire world prison population. The statistics are even more brutal for racial minorities. For example, one out of every 36 African Americans is in prison, with the bulk of the imprisoned black population being young males.

As Sachs points out, this is quite remarkable for a country that never lets up in its criticism of the People's Republic of China for human rights abuses. By way of comparison, the proportion of prisoners in the United States is 30 times higher than in China. The United States would of course argue that the difference between it and China is that the latter routinely uses imprisonment as a way of silencing or otherwise dealing with political dissidents.

That China uses imprisonment as a way of silencing dissidents is well documented and probably beyond question. It does not follow however that the United States never does so. The mere fact that there are so many innocent people in American prisons suggests that there may well be prisoners in the United States who could justifiably be considered political prisoners or at least prisoners of conscience.

It is impossible to know precisely how many such prisoners are languishing in American prisons. The Innocence Project estimates however that between 2.3% and 5% of all prisoners in the U.S. are innocent. In other words between 46000 and 100000 people are improperly imprisoned in the world's most vocal democracy.

The Innocence Project has helped clear may suspects through the use of DNA. This is typically done before the suspect goes to trial. It is impossible to test every person charged with a crime and the persons who are fortunate enough to be tested form only a small percentage of accused persons. More broadly, we know that innocent people are often identified as suspects by law enforcement and that DNA testing often clears them before they go to trial, but that DNA testing is impossible in the vast majority of criminal cases. In 2011/2012 approximately 25% of cases where DNA testing was done by the Federal Bureau of Investigations during the course of criminal investigations, suspects were cleared by the testing. The Innocence Project was very careful however in extrapolating from this, and avoided the assumption that 25% of convictions are in error. Nevertheless they concluded that this figure, "when coupled with the fact that DNA testing is only possible in 5-10% of all criminal cases," showed that even science could not guarantee the absence of unfair convictions.

While the United States is unlikely to imprison a well-known author for his or her writings, the country does nevertheless have an almost unique culture of imprisoning people too casually. The victims of this approach are people seen as not legitimate members of mainstream society. These people are also more likely to be over policed and even summarily executed by police officers. They will certainly serve disproportionately longer sentences for crimes more 'legitimate' members of society may not even be charged for.

This is clearly something that has concerned the Obama administration. Increasingly however even conservative politicians are beginning to suspect that the way racial minorities and low income Americans have been dealt with by the legal system may be inefficient and costly to society.

A report by the organization Vera Institute of Justice called *The Price of Prisons,* found that the average annual cost of incarcerating one inmate in 2012 was $31,286. In New York State, the *per capita* cost was $60,076. These figures were not too different from the numbers released by the *Federal Register: the Daily Journal of the United States Government* showing that the fee to cover the average cost of incarceration for Federal inmates in Fiscal Year 2014 was $30,619.85 or $83.89 per day.

It is interesting to contrast this with the cost of university education. According to the student support organization College Board, published tuition fees for 2014/15 at state colleges was an average of US$9,139 for state residents and $22,958 for everyone else. The average cost at private not for profit colleges was $31,231.

According to the *CBS News* edition of April 23, 2012, this senseless expenditure on incarceration costs the nation $63.4 billion a year.

Richard Nixon could not have foreseen this cost when he boldly declared his war on drugs in 1971. At that time fewer than 40,000 were incarcerated for drug offences. At the time of writing that figure stands at 500,000. The war waged by the Nixon administration was targeted and manifestly unfair.

Although African Americans use drugs at the same rate as white Americans, the former group is incarcerated at a much higher rate. Three out of every four persons incarcerated for drug possession are African Americans. According to Prison

Policy Initiative, the nonpartisan research group, in 2010 there were 2,207 Black prisoners per 100,000 of the population. The figure for Latinos was 966 while the number for Whites was a mere 380.

This fact and the sheer cost of incarcerating people may well have made it easier for the US Justice Department to release about 6,000 inmates early in late 2015. This represented the largest one-time release of federal prisoners in American history. The purpose of the release was to ease jail congestion and provide relief to nonviolent drug offenders. Included in the number of released prisoners were about 2000 foreign nationals who would be deported instead of staying in prison. That of course begs the question; why were they not deported at the time of conviction? The answer perhaps is that the American legal system is robotically casual in the way it imprisons certain people.

The 6000 prisoners released in 2015 were just the first batch. President Obama commuted the sentences of 61 inmates at the end of March 2016 as part of his ongoing effort to give relief to prisoners who were harshly sentenced in the nation's war on drugs. More than one-third of the inmates were serving life sentences. At this point Mr. Obama had granted clemency to 248 federal inmates, in addition to these 61.

In 2014 the US Sentencing Commission reduced the punishment for future drug offenders, which became retroactive. As a result of this change in sentencing guidelines the US Sentencing Commission estimated another 4,600 of the nation's 100,000 drug offenders could be released early. Indeed on May 04, 2016 President Obama commuted the sentences of 58 inmates as part of his ongoing initiative to release federal prisoners who received severe mandatory sentences for non-violent drug offences.

Given the size of the prison population, these changes may appear modest. But it has taken years to reach a point where even conservatives question the value of mass and casual incarceration.

There is a sad historical context to this uniquely American form of incarceration.

Professor Victor E. Kappeler, of the School of Justice Studies at Eastern Kentucky University has traced the birth and development of the American police to the institution of slavery and the control of minorities. Modern police departments were born out of Slave Patrols and Night Watches, which were both designed to control the behaviours of racial minorities. Thus the police force in St. Louis Missouri (less than 13 kilometres from Ferguson where Michael Brown, an unarmed eighteen year old youth was shot by a white officer on August 19, 2014) was founded to protect residents from Native Americans in that frontier city.

The nation's first slave patrol however was developed in South Carolina in 1704. The purpose of this patrol, like all future slave patrols was to help maintain the economic order of the day by assisting wealthy white landowners in recovering and punishing escaped slaves.

In light of this history Sachs argues that the jailing of more than two million people in the United States is an attempt to revive slavery and slave labour. In support of this claim Sachs points to the use of prisoners by American corporations as a 'giant slave labour pool.' The reasoning here is that prisoners are compelled to produce goods extremely cheaply, for the benefit of corporations who go on to sell these goods at high prices. Thus the prisoners are used by corporations in much the same way as slaves were used by white landowners.

The connection between slavery and modern day imprisonment in the United States is a fascinating subject. For our purposes, it suffices to observe that the corruption of the American legal system is not owned by a single individual or institution. This is something that has evolved over time. But its origins were simple enough. Law enforcement agencies were used to pursue most vigorously only certain types of persons. From the enforcers' point of view no harm could come from pursuing these easy targets. And yet a huge amount of societal harm did come, not perhaps immediately but many years later.

Let Zambia be warned that selective and targeted prosecution of suspects in corruption cases could have as devastating consequences for the country as those seen in the United States. To avoid these costly consequences, law enforcement in Zambia must be done professionally, independently, and impartially.

Part Three
The Legacy

CHAPTER ELEVEN

The Essence of Michael Sata

President Michael Sata will be judged by what he did, what he failed to do, and how he behaved. He was a man of contradictions. He was generally a poor listener who nonetheless sought advice from the most unlikely people, and took action on the basis of that advice. His tenure as mayor (governor in *One Party State* parlance) of Lusaka was characterised by decisive leadership and financial prudence but as president he was impulsive and profligate as evidenced by his decision to create new districts and a province, 'with immediate effect' and without consultation. In fairness it should be added that according to the Zambian Auditor-General there was a significant drop in the amount of misappropriated public money after Sata took office. Thus in each of 2010 and 2011 when the MMD was in power, US$200,000 was misappropriated. The amount for 2012, the first year after Sata came to power, was US$92,600. The misspending during the Sata years was on populist projects like unbudgeted pay increases for low income Zambians and unjustified pay increases and perquisites for already privileged government officials.

He was impatient with theory but enjoyed the written word. He was conscientious and compassionate but also silver tongued. He was disciplined but for most of his adult life he was a chain smoker who only kicked the habit after suffering coronary thrombosis. It has to be said that once he was told to give up smoking he never looked back. Sata always accepted the inevitable.

The country knew Sata well and appreciated his work as mayor of Lusaka and effective cabinet minister of both the health and local government ministries. The people were reluctant however to thrust him into the presidency because of concerns about his perceived unpredictability, lack of diplomacy and impatience. He did not come across as a chief executive officer but instead presented as a foreman more comfortable with operations than strategy. But after 20 years of MMD rule, fatigue with the status quo overwhelmed caution and Sata was elected president.

For three years, the nation was led by a man who was tempestuous but too ill to always enforce his will. He was annoyed when kept waiting and stuck relentlessly to routine and protocol when he was well enough to do so.

George Bush's visit to Zambia in July 2012 illustrates the point.

Mr Bush was in the country with his wife Laura to promote the work of their cervical cancer prevention foundation, and paid a courtesy call on President Sata at State House.

Unfortunately the Bushes arrived 15 minutes late. King Cobra, as Sata was popularly known, was not amused. He complained about the former US president being late for the meeting, adding that were the former first couple not bringing money to Zambia, he would not have waited for them. He also dismissed the Bushes' philanthropic work as no more than "payback time for colonialists." In keeping with this theme the Zambian president went on to accuse the United States of abandoning Africa after taking the continent's raw materials to build American cities.

Mr Bush's polite rejoinder that his country never colonised anyone, fell on deaf ears, with the Zambian leader firing back that the United States' role in the transatlantic slave industry made them as culpable as European colonial powers.

Sata's overreaction to the Bushes' tardiness must be seen from the point of view of a Zambian nationalist acutely aware of the casual and disrespectful manner in which African countries are often treated by American and European media. On at least one occasion Sata complained to me about 'imperialist' hubris and lack of respect. On that occasion he was referring to what he saw as automatic condemnation of anything Mr. Robert Mugabe, the Zimbabwean president, did. Sata did not necessarily support Mugabe's policies but he felt duty bound to support a fellow Southern African leader from what he saw as an imperialist onslaught. Sata believed in Zambian sovereignty and was prepared to assert it at the slightest provocation, even when that provocation was more imaginary than real.

Sata's temperament is as much a part of his legacy as the decisions and actions he took while in office. As the above exchange between him and Bush illustrates, personality leaves indelible memories.

CHAPTER TWELVE

Man of Action no More

The Michael Sata sworn in as president of Zambia in 2011 was in many ways a different person from the Michael Sata who bravely abandoned the ruling party in 2001, formed a new political party, and took part in national elections after just a few weeks of campaigning.

Until his departure from the MMD Michael Sata was closely associated with President Frederick Chiluba. Sata's hope was that at the end of Chiluba's term as president, the outgoing president would use his influence to ensure that Sata succeeded him. If that did not work, Sata was prepared to change the republican constitution so that Chiluba could stand for a third term and during that term prepare a smoother transition of power to him.

Although President Chiluba had previously expressed his desire to retire at the end of his second term, the issue continued to dominate debate toward the end of 2000 and at the beginning of 2001. The debate continued because of a large number of political functionaries who feared that Chiluba's departure would also mean the end of their jobs. This group was supported by less visible political operatives who enjoyed immense privileges as a result of Chiluba's presidency.

By the end of 2000 these people had succeeded in weakening Chiluba's resolve to step down after his second term. Chiluba knew however that changing the Zambian constitution and winning the Zambian people over to the third term cause would not be easy. He therefore avoided taking a public stand and instead waged his campaign through proxies.

It was the Movement for Multiparty Democracy spokesman and veteran politician Vernon Johnson Mwaanga who stated publicly in February 2001 that President Chiluba wanted "the issue of a third term to be freely debated."

The unnecessary debate itself had commenced late in 2001 when some MMD leaders in rural areas started the campaign. Among them was one of Zambia's foremost traditional rulers, Paramount Chief Mpezeni, a regular recipient of presidential favour throughout the Chiluba years.

The arguments used by the pro third term camp were typically disingenuous. For example, Northern Province Deputy Minister Daniel Kapapa argued that President Chiluba needed time to complete his programmes. But Chiluba had known from the very first day of his presidency that even if he was re-elected in 1996, he could not serve beyond October 2001. He had had more than ample time within which to plan and implement his programmes.

The Zambian public was not fooled and found the arguments of the third term lobby contemptuous. This opposition was not confined to Chiluba's political opponents. Members of the president's own party took issue with the proposal, calling it an assault on democracy.

Professional people were equally concerned. Sakwiba Sikota, a Lusaka-based lawyer, said: "The whole campaign is clearly orchestrated by Chiluba himself. If he was not interested in running again, he would have re-affirmed his earlier stand."

Within the ruling party the split was glaring. The Copperbelt, Luapula, Central and Eastern (home of Chief Mpezeni) provinces resolved to support the third term bid. But the MMD in Lusaka province opposed it.

This set the MMD national secretary Michael Sata, and the party's chairman for elections Ackson Sejani, who saw the proposal as an assault on democracy, on a collision course. Sata was not going to back down easily. He told a pro-Chiluba rally: "We will petition the president to stand. Those resolutions made by Lusaka province are wishful thinking of the new executive and those with wishful thinking are in the minority."

In the end, of course, Chiluba backed down and arranged for Mwanawasa to succeed him. Thus Sata's plan to succeed Chiluba immediately or after Chiluba had served a third term, came to nothing.

The future president's only option now was to form his own party and compete in elections scheduled for 27 December 2001. In order to do so, Sata had to transform himself very quickly. Hitherto he had been Chiluba's "Mr. Fix it" and now he was a presidential candidate against Chiluba's party. He set about to underplay his rough side and emphasise his more thoughtful side. In an interview with the British born, Zambian raised BBC correspondent Penny Dale, Sata described himself as "a very nice man, a very kind man but someone who brooks no nonsense".

It was important for Sata to cultivate this image. The country wanted a tough and disciplined leader but they did not want a thug, which is what some of Sata's critics claimed he was. The respected Zambian sociologist, Owen Sichone saw Sata's qualities in the following way: "He is not good for democracy but he can whip and bully a drunken and demoralised Zambia into action." Sichone also saw Sata's immediate challenge in changing his image. "His biggest problem is his MMD career. Having been used to destroy some good people's careers, he now finds himself with a few weeks in which to rebuild his image."

Sichone was not alone in recognising Sata as a man of action. Indeed *A man of action* was Sata's campaign slogan.

The phrase resonated with everyone who knew him, including detractors.

Almost everyone I talked to at the time said Sata knew how to get a job done, but they all worried about what the cost of getting the job done might be. They could only hope, as Guy Scott, Sata's future vice president did, that he would "use technocrats who perform and [not feel] insecure if someone knows better."

Curiously, Scott went on to add:

> He's an odd mixture and hard to read. He cultivates a rough image but he's truly concerned about people's suffering - perhaps that's what makes him charismatic.

In late 2001 the people of Zambia found Sata hard to read and were not yet persuaded that he was the one to alleviate their suffering. In the short period he had to campaign, it is perhaps not surprising that the PF received only 3.4 per cent of the vote. On this occasion the Boat, symbol of the new party, failed to deliver electoral success.

Nonetheless Guy Scott was correct to observe that Michael Sata was concerned about people's suffering. Even when he was not campaigning for office Sata could be relied upon to help a neighbour (and he defined that term very broadly) who was bereaved or facing other challenges.

Sata never distanced himself from the poor and humble. He actually maintained relations with the humblest of people even after he became president. I remember once sitting in the ante room to his office at State House when a call came in from a high density residential area known as Chilenje. The secretary picked up the phone and asked who was calling. "Which Mr. Phiri?" the secretary enquired further. It was clear from what I could hear that this was a low income person who would not normally fraternise with powerful politicians but who felt confident Sata would have time for him. I was just wondering how the president who already had a number of people waiting to see him would react. I was pleasantly surprised when the secretary told the caller that the president would speak to him immediately.

Sata was instinctively a man of the people. Unfortunately as president he not only missed the opportunity to end corruption but also the opportunity to create a people's economy that would have maximised employment for the people he cared so much about.

While employment in the formal sector did rise by 58,000 in the first nine months of 2013, the Sata government could have created many more jobs had Sata been more focused than he was and less ill. There were certain things Sata could have done to whip the nation into action, as predicted by Sichone. Sata was a patriot who genuinely wanted to see ordinary people do well economically.

He was precisely the kind of leader who would have been bold enough to use government procurement, for example, as a way of empowering ordinary Zambians.

The following section shows how this could have been done.

Michael Sata sworn in as Zambia's fifth president

CHAPTER THIRTEEN

The Economy Waiting to be created

Few politicians understood the importance of by-laws better than Sata who had served both as mayor of Lusaka and as cabinet minister responsible for local government. And yet Sata allowed unlicensed street vendors to continue operating in all major Zambian cities to the detriment of legitimate business people. The argument that illegal street vending could not be stopped as that would deprive thousands of Zambians of a livelihood was unimaginative. In addition to undermining order, this argument let the government off the hook in its duty to set the stage for sustainable employment for illegal vendors.

Sata should have understood that through enforcement of by-laws and regulations that aid the conduct of orderly business and through practical and people-focused procurement policy, Zambia could (and can) create the basis for a dynamic new economy.

In the longer term, many illegal street vendors will need basic education and skills training. There are however steps that Sata could have taken almost immediately upon assuming office that could have resulted in immediate economic improvement for citizens and set the stage for spectacular growth in the future. Sata had the personality to challenge many assumptions the country makes about development. He also had enough private sector experience to understand market signals.

Road Construction

For example, the assumption is almost always made that all road construction requires huge capital outlays and the involvement of large corporations. While this may be true for trunk roads, it is not always true with respect to community roads. Most community roads in Zambia are no more than paths created by sheer usage over time. These paths are in fact a signal from the market that people need a road. They are also an opportunity for labour intensive construction of community roads.

Consider this example from South Africa. The Amadiba community of Eastern Cape Province was given an opportunity to construct a six-metre wide and forty-kilometre long road that connected the community in OR Tambo District to a trunk road. The immediate effect of constructing the road was to create employment, mostly short term, in a community where 75 per cent of the population was unemployed. About 60 per cent of the newly-employed were women. The road construction uplifted community spirit and generated huge optimism. This is evident from the perceptions that the community recorded about the impact of the project on the quality of life. A subsequent survey by M Mashiri, D Thevadasan, and R Zukulu revealed high levels of satisfaction with the impact of the project on the community. Thus all respondents thought travel to main settlements had improved. No one thought it had deteriorated. Perhaps that is to be expected. Less obvious was the finding that 96.6 per cent of respondents thought local clinic visitation had improved with only 3.4 per cent disagreeing, and 93.1 per cent thought access to community centres had improved while 6.9 per cent disagreed.

In addition to the temporary jobs created, there were also marketable skills developed and some villagers went on to become construction supervisors with an opportunity to obtain permanent employment. Small businesses in the community also reported an increase in trade especially during the construction period. Altogether this remote community saw a decline in poverty rates and an increase in communal capacity.

There are many communities in Zambia that would benefit from labour intensive road construction whose beneficial attributes include cost effectiveness and employment generation. The International Labour Organization estimates that labour intensive road construction is between 10 and 30 per cent cheaper than capital intensive road construction.

Anyone driving on the main road from the Copperbelt to Lusaka will be struck by the number of makeshift markets along the way. These trading centres, which operate illegally, are in fact connected to villages and other communities that produce the items they sell.

Collaboration between communities, local authorities, central government, and the private sector could result in the formalisation of these markets for the benefit of the communities and the country.

A number of communities close to the Ndola/Kabwe road would be prime candidates for this proposal. For any one of them, the first step might be the construction of a labour intensive road from the supplier communities to the roadside markets. The relatively low cost of construction would be borne by both the local authority and the central government. The signal from the market in this instance is twofold - construction of a road to service the community, and establishment of a well serviced roadside trading post that includes facilities like public toilets and parking space. So, the makeshift market must be replaced by a safe, modern and properly serviced roadside facility. The new market must of course comply with planning by-laws, in addition to being aesthetically pleasing.

The new roadside market would now be operated by entrepreneurs leasing appropriately constructed stalls from the local authority. Community suppliers would sell to regulated traders in the formal sector and expect a fair price for their produce. More travellers would stop over because of increased safety, parking, and facilities like well serviced toilets. This would of course increase the likelihood of travellers buying from the market. In these circumstances it would make sense to enforce laws against illegal and nuisance traders in unauthorised areas. The reduction in illegal trading would eliminate unfair competition for legitimate businesses and increase their profits which in turn would increase revenue flows to the local authority in the form of fees from the lease of stalls.

The investment originally made in the construction of the road by the local authority would yield a return not only in the form of fees for stalls but possibly also from property taxes payable on the value of privately owned but publicly serviced permanent structures at the roadside market. The return to both the local authority and the central government is the increased wealth in the community as well as the creation of a safer roadside market.

For the private sector, an opportunity to trade fairly and raise capital over the longer term is created.

And of course the community wins in a big way by being able to transport its produce in larger volume to an expanding clientele. Furthermore, the community has access to both short term and longer term employment because even after the labour intensive construction has ended, the new roadside market will require parking attendants, janitors, cleaners and other employees.

Encouraging communities to build feeder roads for themselves allows large construction companies to concentrate on bigger projects such as trunk roads. Typically, the Zambian government turns to donors whenever a need for construction or maintenance of a trunk road is identified. In fact foreign aid is not the only way of constructing trunk roads. The local private sector can play a useful role in building the road network that Zambia so badly needs.

The opportunity for participation by small and medium sized companies with ties to communities is immense given the fact that there are an estimated 30,000 km of unofficial community roads comprising of trails, tracks and footpaths.

For larger companies, there are opportunities too as the PF government appears to have followed MMD Finance Minister Situmbeko Musokotwane's announcement in mid-2010 that his government had plans to significantly expand the country's infrastructure by investing in a number of projects including roads, airports, border posts, farming blocks, power generation, transport and housing units. This was going to be done through what he called 'public private arrangements.'

In order to manage bulk commercial traffic, the PF government has purported to encourage the private sector to invest in toll road construction based on sustainable revenue models.

Unfortunately the way these arrangements with the private sector would work is not clear and it may not be axiomatic that an invitation to foreign investors to participate in road construction will be followed immediately by positive investor participation. Zambia continues to be mistrusted by many potential foreign investors following the unilateral cancellation of mining development agreements in 2008. It was on the basis of these agreements that mining companies raised foreign capital to invest in Zambia's then ailing mining industry. Michael Sata had an opportunity to reverse this decision and honourably negotiate new development agreements. He never did.

But this bad episode in the country's recent history is beginning to fade and the Lungu government appears genuine in its efforts to reach out to potential foreign investors. In the circumstances it is worth pursuing other ways of constructing roads by utilization of international commercial connections.

It is clear to all that the main trunk road connecting Livingstone town in the South to Chililabombwe in the Copperbelt province is no longer adequate for the transportation of people and goods from one end of the country to the other. While traffic has expanded greatly in recent years, this road's capacity to handle more vehicles has not grown.

A business case for the construction of a new dual carriageway from Livingstone (preferably via Chirundu) to Chililabombwe can easily be made. The Livingstone to Chililabombwe road is the main transportation artery in the country, moving not just passengers but varied goods like copper cathodes, heavy equipment, food etc.

In order to develop further this very important artery, the government could post an international tender for the construction of the carriageway as a toll road. The tender would be of interest to companies at home and abroad wishing to invest in Zambia for the longer term. The likely outcome is that a consortium of Zambian and foreign interests would emerge to construct the dual carriageway. Zambia's ability to attract this kind of long term investment would at least in part depend on the country's reputation at the time as a reliable destination of foreign direct investment with a commitment to the rule of law and a credible dispute settlement mechanism. If these conditions were satisfied, Zambia could see the construction of a high quality road completed in short order for the benefit of both the country and the investors.

The building of the road would not however be the end of the story. Opportunities would also be created for Zambian entrepreneurs to start businesses such as filling stations along the new road. The government too would have an opportunity to serve more people through facilities like health and recreation centres for the use of motorists and communities living near the new road.

Local Government

The City of Ndola, like other towns on the Copperbelt, has a lovely aerial view suggesting well laid out streets. The reality however is that visitors to the city have great difficulty finding their way around because most streets no longer have name signs. The signs have fallen off and the local authority has done little to repair or replace them.

When asked why the city has no signage, the officials' knee jerk response is that there is no money. In fact it is not the lack of money that is responsible for this; it is lack of innovation and a reluctance to think outside the box.

While streets remain unsigned in much of Ndola, the city also boasts an informal sector with some of the best sign makers in the business. The young men engaged in the trade typically serve motorists requiring number plates and road safety triangles. They are lucky to take home $10 after a hard day's work, and often earn less than that. Assuming the council contracted these sign makers at least once a year to work as independent contractors on two hundred streets for an average fee of $100 per street and assigned one sign maker to work on 10 streets, a total of 20 sign makers would be employed at a cost of $20,000. Thereafter the council would call upon the sign makers as the need arose and would use them as part of an overall street maintenance plan. The street sign makers would of course continue to do other work such as car number plate signage, building signage etc. But being given work by the council, however seasonal, would make the business of sign making more sustainable and have the effect of increasing income in the community, as each contracted worker would potentially qualify for membership in the Zambian middle class. The African Development Bank uses consumption expenditure of between $2 and $20 a day to define the middle class. That threshold would be met comfortably by the sign makers.

The cost of $20,000 a year to sort out the street signage problem in Ndola is easily affordable. It is significantly less than the $33,000 earmarked for councillors' allowances in the 2015 Ndola City Council budget of roughly US$11 million. Of this, 27.1 per cent was earmarked for service provision, and 8.2 per cent for Ward and Constituency development. 64.7 per cent was earmarked for personal emoluments, councillors' allowances, and administration.

It seems clear from the pattern of expenditure that the council needs to have better priorities. Clearly, the council needs to cut its emoluments and administration bill and use the money saved to fund services and infrastructure development which will in turn aid private sector job creation.

A well thought out plan to keep Ndola clean could also have the same salutary effect of aiding private sector job creation if garbage collection and related activities were contracted out to qualified members of the public.

The passage of the Constitution of Zambia (Amendment) Act 2016 provides a huge opportunity for this kind of innovation to take place. The new constitution creates the position of mayor with executive powers, elected for a maximum of two five year terms. This fact alone will encourage mayors to look at proposals whose effect is to increase employment levels and beautify the city.

City Parking is Big Business

Perhaps the best opportunity for generating jobs in Zambia's cities lies in the labour intensive parking system I proposed in 1991. The plan was subsequently shared with Dr Silane Mwenechanya, one of Zambia's leading business, and legal consultants, in the mid-1990s. His assessment was that the plan's strength lay in its simplicity. He also made suggestions as to how the plan could be adapted to existing socioeconomic reality.

In early 1991 I was asked to go to Zambia to help the Bank of Zambia, then under the able leadership of Canadian central banker Jacques Bussières, to do a study on the development of a viable money market in the country. Bussières understood my view that a viable money market could not be developed without the active participation of local authorities, since they were (at different times) both potential borrowers and potential lenders. But before the creation of any market a way had to be found to increase local governments' ability to raise revenue.

To illustrate how this could be done I looked at ways in which parking in Lusaka could be made profitable for the local authority. Lusaka had 100,000 parking spaces, and I believed the city council could reasonably expect a return per day of $1 on each space. The combined potential income of all these places would thus be $100,000 a day. Unlike other parking systems however, no parking meters would be installed. Instead there would be a parking attendant with responsibility for ten cars. The attendant's duties would include issuance of parking tickets and ensuring that each parked car had a sticker indicating payment for that day. To avoid attendants carrying too much cash, arrangements would be made with a local bank to provide mobile banking services. (A Zambian owned bank with whom the plan was shared expressed an interest in providing the mobile banking service.) Mobile phone payments would today reduce the risk of the parking attendant carrying too much cash.

For every ten attendants there would be an inspector who would manage the front line workers.

The 1991 study suggested that the attendants be paid twice the going rate for security guards employed by diplomatic missions in Zambia. The inspectors would earn twice the pay of attendants. In addition to personnel, the parking system would require a modest office and a couple of tow trucks and mobile communication devices. Uniforms would be another cost. Today tow trucks may well be unnecessary given advances in car wheel clamp technology. This would increase the profitability of the business.

Taking all foreseeable expenses into account the study's preliminary finding was that a pre-tax profit of $5,000,000 per annum was realisable from this venture. Dr Mwenechanya and I agreed that the business should not be run by the council but by private concerns. Dr Mwenechanya favoured a system that offered the ten spaces to individual entrepreneurs. I favoured a concession of the whole system to a reputable company chosen after a competitive tender.

We consulted Lusaka City Council as we fine-tuned the proposal. Unfortunately the council had little appreciation of the detail but were seduced by the potential to make money, and in clear violation of intellectual property laws and business ethics, implemented the proposal without our knowledge, hoping to keep the projected $5million profit. Not surprisingly, the scheme failed. The success of the system depended on it being operated in accordance with the principles of market economics, with concomitant discipline. Whether operated by one large company or a number of individual entrepreneurs, Dr Mwenechanya and I had envisaged the operators taking the risk and being rewarded with an annual profit of $5million. The city council would then receive an annual concession fee of $1million per annum, without the headache of running the business.

But the benefit to society as a whole would go beyond the concession fee paid to the council, as 10,000 new jobs for young people would be created. These young people would earn enough to pay council levies and possibly income tax. They would then go on to spend the money they earned and help maintain or create new jobs in the rest of the economy. Furthermore, with each car under the watchful eye of an attendant, security in Lusaka would be greatly improved as car thefts declined.

A decade after my study, the Cape Town City Council adopted a similar system to regulate parking in the central business district.

Kent Morkel, the Council's Executive Committee member responsible for Economic Development, Tourism and Property, welcomed the decision as a major step in the city's drive to provide a safe, clean environment. He saw the system as evidence of how public and private sectors can cooperate for the common good. He also thought well-regulated parking for both residents and visitors helped Cape Town to be globally competitive and attractive to tourists.

Despite the Sata government's failure to encourage ventures such as this, a young Zambian Canadian entrepreneur, Kaluba Chilaisha, relocated to Zambia to try out the 1991 proposal. He formed a company called Dante Investments Limited, whose special purpose vehicle, City Parking Solutions, then formed a partnership with Servest of South Africa to run a parking system for the City of Ndola. Chilaisha identified two major impediments to starting the project. The first was financing for a new idea. The banks in Zambia were extremely reluctant to support a business that did not fit their usual profile. The second impediment was a culture that is suspicious of and resistant to new ideas. In the end however the young entrepreneur did change some minds and the business took off. Dante entered into a seven year contract with the City Council of Ndola to manage 1,100 parking bays and 200 slots.

The fee charged for parking, at 2 Kwacha (roughly 16 cents) per 30 minutes is well below the $1 threshold suggested for Lusaka in the 1991 study. Even so, the project has been beneficial to Dante, the City and the community. The company earns about $600 a day.

The City gets 30 per cent of net income per month or 30 per cent of $4,166, whichever is greater. Dante has a site manager and 80 local employees. Chilaisha describes his site manager, Mutepa Puta, as "reliable, smart and dependable."

At the time of writing Dante is in negotiations with the cities of Lusaka and Kitwe as well as the University of Zambia and the University Teaching Hospital to run similar parking systems.

Enforcing By-Laws

Entrepreneurial ventures like the City Parking Solutions system are necessary to place Zambia on the path to prosperity. These ventures are more likely to thrive however in an orderly environment rather than a chaotic one because there is an economic dividend that comes from order. Put simply, enforcing council by-laws is critical to sustainable development.

For example, by-laws require all households in municipalities to be well maintained and in a hygienic manner. There is even a legal expectation that houses will be painted at frequent intervals. Some by-laws actually require home occupants to maintain manicured lawns. If local authorities announced their intention to enforce these by-laws and actually demonstrated their willingness to take action against households disregarding the law, a market would soon develop for the provision of gardening and other property maintenance services.

The very nature of the work would ensure that these services were provided by local companies and thus an opportunity would be created to increase community wealth, with the usual multiplier effect in the rest of the economy. Furthermore, local authorities would have to lead by example. They could not reasonably expect householders to obey the law when they themselves did not. So, local governments would have to ensure that areas zoned as parks were treated as such and actually maintained (ideally by private concerns) as parks for everyone's enjoyment. The principle would also apply to maintenance of cemeteries, public libraries, public toilets and other public buildings.

In addition to the salutary economic effects, enforcing by-laws would also aid the creation of healthy communities. This is something President Mwanawasa understood. In launching his Keep Zambia Clean and Healthy campaign in 2007, Mwanawasa's local government ministry identified many advantages of cleanliness and good hygiene practices in the home, community, and workplace. According to the ministry, the benefits are not only economic but also 'physical and psychological.'

The Secretariat of the *Keep Zambia Clean and Healthy Programme* described the benefits in the launch document as follows:

> Good personal hygiene not only makes us look and feel better about ourselves, it also helps prevent skin infections, scabies, lice, gum and tooth disease and a whole host of other infectious diseases. A clean home and surroundings, where the yard is swept, rubbish removed, and water protected will be a far happier and healthier place for children, than one that is unkempt.

The Secretariat went on to extol the virtues of a business or workplace with a clean environment. Not only does a hygienic environment contribute to a reduction in employee absence through illness with its negative effect on productivity and business costs, it provides an attractive environment that makes staff feel and perform better. Productivity increases and the business benefits.

It is regrettable that no clear leadership on this matter has been shown since the demise of Mr Mwanawasa. It is especially regrettable that Michael Sata (whose example as mayor of Lusaka Mwanawasa was actually following) never showed visible leadership in executing this worthwhile initiative.

Seven years after the launch of the initiative, the Sata Government expressed disappointment with the way the Keep Zambia Clean and Healthy campaign was being implemented.

The Local Government and Housing Minister, Emerine Kabanshi, identified garbage collection as one area that had not performed well because "most local authorities lack capacity to effectively clear refuse."

In the kind of economy the public would have expected President Sata to create this would be the kind of function that would be contracted to private entities with a view to generating employment and prosperity. Sata was the kind of leader who would have ignored political considerations and side lined obstructionist politicians when satisfied that the public good demanded it.

Procurement

The extent to which the political leadership can be sidestepped is unfortunately limited in a country like Zambia with a history of an unduly dominant state.

Procurement as a tool for economic regeneration cannot succeed without a conscious effort on the part of the government to increase opportunities for nationals.

I spoke to President Sata about this in November 2013. It was clear to me then that his capacity to absorb new information had greatly diminished since assuming the presidency. Ideas that would have excited him as leader of the opposition no longer did.

We must rely on future governments to adopt policies that oblige the Zambian government to only consume good and services that have Zambian content. It may well be necessary to have exceptions to this rule but in that event the exceptions should never be allowed to become the norm.

The business sector should be given a timeframe within which to increase local content in goods and services consumed by the government. This policy need not affect consumption patterns in the private sector - its purpose would be to use government as a vehicle for the promotion of Zambian entrepreneurship.

Let's imagine that on April 1, 2017, the government of Zambia announced that with effect from June the following year it would not ordinarily consume goods and services that did not have local content. The amount of content would depend on the particular item. In the case of motor vehicles, for example, it might suffice, at least in the early years of the policy, to simply assemble the vehicles locally. On the other hand, packaged food consumed by institutions like the army, might need a local content level of say 60 per cent. Products already made in Zambia would of course qualify for purchase and consumption by government.

It is estimated that each year the Zambian government imports about 9,000 vehicles for its various arms. The exact number is difficult to ascertain because many of these vehicles are bought for the intelligence network which is unwilling to divulge details of its purchases. Officials at the Road Transport and Safety Agency in Lusaka did assure me however that the figure of 9,000 was conservative.

If Zambia were to announce that these vehicles would henceforth have to be assembled in Zambia, and that in future they would be required to have a certain amount of local content, the country would probably be inundated with offers from vehicle manufacturers wishing to 'corner' the Zambian market by setting up a local assembly plant. The car makers' hope would be to sell cars to the broader national and regional market, using the 9,000 government vehicles as a guaranteed market.

The proper way to determine who eventually is allowed to set up the assembly plant would be by way of public tender with the process stipulating the conditions of maximum employment for Zambians, and a commitment to use Zambian-made products in the manufacturing process.

The extent to which the assembly plant was automated would depend on a combination of factors including the preferences of the investor. The Chrysler Assembly Plant in Belvidere, Illinois, for example, has 3,400 employees and 900 robots working around the clock, in three shifts, to build cars.

In general however, a modern highly automated plant requires an average of three people to produce one car. So, even if our assembly plant was unable to supply the general public and regional consumers, potentially 27,000 Zambians would secure employment. The number of employees would be even higher if the plant was less automated but we shall assume our plant is as automated as the average North American plant.

Real (Ray) Tanguay, Chairman of Toyota Canadian Operations and President of Canadian Auto Parts Toyota Inc. from 2010 to 2015 has estimated that for every job created in the car industry, between five and seven jobs are created in the broader economy. Conservatively then it can be estimated that a policy on the part of the government to only buy motor vehicles assembled in Zambia would result not only in the direct employment of as many as 27,000 Zambians (depending on the size of the expatriate contingent deemed necessary by the assembly plant owner), but would also result in 135,000 jobs being created in the broader economy. In reality the figure would be even higher because the vehicles assembled locally would be purchased by the Zambian private sector too and possibly other consumers in the Southern African region, which would all add to demand for labour in the industry.

The multiplier effect in the motor vehicle industry is not unique to North America. It is also true in Europe where the automotive industry is seen as the engine of the economy, with one in ten jobs being dependent directly or indirectly on it. According to the European Automobile Manufacturers Association the industry is also the largest investor in innovation and research and development and of course the driver of European exports. In the United States the automotive sector spent $102 billion on research and development in 2013.

When it is performing well, the industry has a huge positive impact on the wider economy because of the thousands of small and medium sized companies involved in the supply chain, vehicle sales and after-sales services.

Zambia could, by intelligent use of the procurement process, develop a healthy automotive industry with a clear role to play in the effort of leading the country to sustainable prosperity. The automotive industry, reliant as it is on successful research and development, could also contribute to establishment of excellence in institutions of higher learning.

Government institutions can also be used to encourage the development of more basic skills. For example, there appears to be a surprisingly large number of underemployed but competent tailors in most Zambian townships and even some villages. Subject to compliance with the established standard, these tailors should be given the opportunity to compete for contracts for the manufacture of uniforms for police officers, customs officers, soldiers and other public officers.

According to published figures, the Zambian armed forces employ 22,000 people. If on average it costs $200 a year to properly clothe each member of the armed forces, then there is $4.4 million dollars' worth of work that could be given to tailors across Zambia. This estimate is far from extravagant and in reality is conservative. The cost of dressing one soldier per annum is likely to be greater than $200. Consider for example that the standard initial clothing allowance for one male soldier in the United States army for the period October 01, 2015 to September 30, 2016 is $1,643 while the allowance for a female soldier stands at $1,888. The respective figures for the Air Force are $1,389.18 and $1,597.93. In the army, the initial allowance is followed on the anniversary month by a standard cash clothing replacement allowance of $468 for males and $469 for women. The respective amounts for the US Air Force are $352 and $360. (*Military Benefits* 2016)

A direct injection of $4.4 million into Zambian communities would have a huge multiplier effect.

And this exercise need not be confined to the provision of uniforms.

Institutions like the army, air force, police service, prisons department, and schools, are all potentially big consumers of packaged food. At the moment they consume far less than they could. This is because Zambia has not done a good job of preserving the food it produces.

I remember once driving from Chingola to Lusaka during a time of drought. Even at that time however I noticed mountains of potatoes at makeshift markets. So abundant was the produce that one could have assumed that the much discussed drought was a figment of official imagination. In fact the drought was real but the shortage of rain was concentrated in the Southern Province, the traditional leader in maize production. Had Zambia invested in a viable food transportation and preservation system, the drought would not have had the impact it did because the country would have been able to transport food from the surplus areas to the deficit areas, and would also have been able to preserve that food for consumption in the post-harvest months.

Food preservation would be aided by an invitation to Zambian entrepreneurs to participate in public tenders for the provision of food to government institutions. Knowing that they had a ready market, entrepreneurs would find a way of preserving food for distribution and sale throughout the year.

This would end the frequent and sad phenomena of food wastage during harvest times and food shortages for the rest of the year.

The majority of this wastage comes from limited access to viable markets and lack of refrigeration and other means of preserving food on a large scale. In other words, most food is lost in Zambia because of food knowledge deficits and poverty.

This need not be the case. Traditional Zambia had ways of preserving food that could be relevant even today. Appropriate and inexpensive modern technology can also be used to increase Zambian capacity to preserve food. The ability to get food to the markets and to preserve food not needed for immediate consumption, would have positive impacts on small scale farmers and their communities. These communities would be better placed to guarantee food for domestic consumption, in addition to increasing their income.

The most common method of preserving food in traditional Zambian society was sun drying. In earlier less polluted times with predictable weather patterns, this worked reasonably well. In much of Zambia, this method would be problematic today because the produce so preserved would be open to contamination by dust and the whole process would depend totally on good weather. In addition the slow drying rates from this method would raise the danger of mould.

The obvious advantage of sun drying is its affordability. For this reason Zambia should be interested in improved methods of sun drying that do not carry the disadvantages indicated above.

One such method is solar drying. Solar dryers are inexpensive, easy to construct and have many advantages over traditional sun drying. For example, solar dryers have higher drying temperatures, resulting in quicker drying. Furthermore, the concern of contamination by dust is addressed since the solar dryer is covered.

They consist of a transparent panel above a black chamber or collector that absorbs heat from the sun. The panel is glazed with a very cheap but tough plastic, polythene. More expensive plastic films with a life span of five or more years can also be used in place of polythene which does not last as long.

This technology has recently been put to good use in India, one of the world's hungriest countries. India in fact leads the world in the number of malnourished people. Despite this, India wastes a huge amount of food. Thus, of the 220 million tons of vegetables and fruit produced in the country, only 70 per cent is actually consumed.

With one third of the country living beyond the grid, many people in India have no electricity to power refrigerators and freezers, leaving them with the choice of either consuming all fresh food immediately or letting it go to waste. And in the absence of refrigerated trucks the food cannot be transported to food deficit areas either.

In 2013, Ben Schiller, an advocate of sustainable business wrote an uplifting piece about Vaibhav Tidke, a 26-year-old doctoral student from Mumbai, who was determined to find a viable solution to food wastage. Concerned about food wastage resulting from lack of storage infrastructure, particularly at harvest-time, Tidke and his colleague Shital Somani commenced a project to produce a low-cost solar device that helped farmers store up to three tons of food a year.

It helped that Tidke himself came from a farming family.

"I visited one of the farms, and I saw that during a particular season of harvesting, fruits and vegetables were really cheap. There was a lot of supply, and much less demand. The farmer didn't have a way of preserving fruit and vegetables," he explained to Schiller.

The solar dryer that Tidke and his colleague designed was very much like the solar device described above. The device takes just a few hours to dry a load of washed and cut fruit and vegetables. The produce so dried retains its colour and texture but it does of course lose some volume. At the time of consumption the items are rehydrated by adding water again. The device works equally well for fish or meat.

The upfront charge for the device is about $57, with virtually no operating costs. It is not surprising therefore that within weeks of launching the product Tidke and Somani sold 50 units, with an expectation of selling 1,000 in the following four months. The long term goal was to distribute 1 million units by 2020. There was also a plan to ship 50 units to Kenya in October 2013.

Canning on a small or large scale is also something that can be done easily. A small scale canning kit will cost as little as $70 while an industrial canning plant may cost millions.

Communities and entrepreneurs will have to decide what the requirements may be in particular circumstances. But before this happens the government must signal its readiness to address the issue of food wastage and put in place the necessary incentives to galvanise the private sector.

Another area that requires immediate government direction is the furniture industry. Visitors to Zambia are often surprised at the quality of furniture made by craftspeople without much formal training. But the standard is inconsistent as there are other woodworkers who are less skilled but who are nonetheless allowed to sell their product; thanks to the government's failure to enforce laws on the quality of manufactured furniture. This industry has potential for growth but it is important for the government to regulate it with a view to guaranteeing quality and manufacturers' effective participation in the formal economy.

The first step perhaps is to enforce by-laws that prohibit roadside trading which is where most of the locally manufactured furniture is sold. This should be followed by an offer of space for the sale of furniture at designated premises zoned for commercial use.

As long as the government and local authorities enforce the law relating to zoning and commerce, legitimate furniture manufacturers will move to the right areas for business, knowing that illegitimate traders will not be permitted to have an unfair advantage by plying their trade illegally along busy roads.

Once by-laws and zoning regulations have been enforced, the government should establish quality standards for the industry and make it mandatory for industry participants to follow these standards.

Critically the government should then undertake only to buy furniture made locally and in accordance with established quality standards. In this way, court house furniture, school desks, home furniture for government officials, furniture in police stations, furniture in security service offices, and anywhere else the government is obliged to furnish, would be made locally. Of course in order to supply this furniture, the manufacturer and seller would be required to register as business entities and be liable to pay tax. The decision to procure furniture from local producers would not only raise incomes and fortify the Zambian middle class; it would also increase revenue to the exchequer, without increasing tax rates.

People's Tourist Sector

Zambia did have an opportunity to provide leadership in global tourism under President Sata. And Zambia did on this occasion acquit herself well.

At the official opening of the United Nations World Tourism conference on August 25, 2013, Secretary General, Taleb Rifai described the conference as the best attended in the history of the organisation, with a record 900 media delegates, 121 full delegates from the member states, 140 delegates from all over the world, 49 foreign ministers and 750 other delegates participating in the event.

Addressing guests during the official opening of the 20th session of the UNWTO general assembly, the Secretary-General expressed his appreciation for what he described as "the immense effort" on the part of Zambia and Zimbabwe, the host countries.

President Sata also congratulated the two co-host countries for their hard work and added that the event was clear testimony of Zambia and Zimbabwe's commitment to exploiting regional tourism.

This was in line with the UNWTO secretary general's vision of promoting tourism growth in sub Saharan Africa, a region projected to have 134 million visitors by 2030.

It is certainly desirable for Zambia and other countries in the region to have more tourists. It is even more important however that Zambians participate fully in local tourism. The starting point is expansion of the Zambian middle class which would have the effect of increasing demand for services provided by the tourist industry. Tourism is too often seen in Zambia as a service only for foreigners. In the new Zambian economy tourism would be seen as a service as much for local people as for foreigners. This should be reflected in both the provision and consumption of tourist services. For while Zambians may have the desire to visit and enjoy sites in their country they may not always feel welcome by operators (both local and foreign) who place a higher value on foreigners. There are complex psychological and sociological reasons why so many formerly subjugated people behave in this fashion. This mentality however can be corrected with appropriate training.

This is just one reason why Zambia has lost many opportunities in promoting tourism to local consumers. While the country has world class resorts such as the hotels in Livingstone, these facilities cater mostly to foreigners partly because of the relatively small size of the Zambian middle class able to afford these excellent facilities. Increasing the size of the Zambian middle class will necessarily increase the number of Zambian tourists enjoying these facilities. But all tourists need more choice than is currently on offer. There are relatively inexpensive ways of expanding choice for both local and foreign visitors.

A visitor to the Livingstone Railway Museum will be impressed by the official guide's knowledge of the history of railways. The visitor will also be saddened by the dilapidated state of the two railway passenger coaches on display. The wooden floors of the coaches have largely been eaten away by termites and are liable to collapse, so the few visitors who go to the museum have to tread carefully as the staff hope that no expensive lawsuit will arise from their employer's negligence. The work needed to restore these lovely coaches can be performed by the nearby Livingstone Trades Training Institute. The request has never been made however because the museum has never felt able to pay for the repairs. It certainly cannot raise enough money from the fee of around one dollar charged for entry to the site.

The museum is in fact a potential financial success. There are clubs for railway enthusiasts all over the world, including in the United Kingdom, United States, Canada, Australia, New Zealand and India. Although there are railway enthusiasts in Zambia they do not yet appear to have formed themselves into a club. The Livingstone Railway Museum would be a delight not only for local train enthusiasts but also for the tens of thousands of steam train fans who belong to these international clubs.

The museum not only houses an exhibit of memorabilia and photographs of the early days in Livingstone, it is also home to nineteenth century steam locomotives, and the vintage railway coaches referred to earlier. But unlike the coaches, the steam locomotives seem to be in reasonably good shape.

The coaches could be refurbished however and turned into theme and period accommodation for tourists with a particular interest in railways. Assuming two refurbished coaches comfortably accommodated twenty tourists, even a relatively small tariff of $50 a night would contribute significantly to the earnings of the Livingstone Railway Museum. Medium cost hotels in Livingstone are scarce and consequently have a high occupancy rate. Assuming a relatively low occupancy rate of eighty per cent, the museum would bring in $292,000 just from this line of business. This would not however be the only source of revenue for the museum, now converted to a hotel museum; revenue would also come from food and drink, preferably served in a vintage coach.

In due course the museum could use its increased revenue to leverage financing for the construction of a world class theme-based hotel, thereby freeing the vintage coaches for non-residential Zambian and foreign visitors.

With the internet, advertising the new facility would be extremely easy, especially if the main strategy employed was targeting railway clubs around the world, all of whom have active websites.

Revamping the Livingstone Railway Museum would increase choices and provide inexpensive accommodation for both local and foreign tourists. It would also provide opportunities for local entrepreneurs who would be involved in the rehabilitation of the vintage coaches, construction of the new facilities, and supply of food and drink.

Opportunities to involve the community in this way are in fact abundant in Zambia. Some of these opportunities like the development of the Shiwa Ng'andu estate in northern Zambia are obvious and have already been successfully exploited. Others are less obvious but no less potentially lucrative.

Many Zambians are aware of the writer Wilbur Smith but few seem to realise that the famed author whose works have been translated into 26 languages, is a fellow national. Wilbur Addison Smith was born on January 9, 1933 in the central mining town of Kabwe. Although Smith has not lived in Zambia for many years he has never forgotten his heritage as evidenced by the fact that most of his writings involve the history of his homeland and Southern Africa.

Wilbur Smith has a huge international following that would be interested in visiting the land of his birth. The house Smith was born in should be turned into a heritage building accessible to his many fans around the world. As far as possible it should be restored to its original condition. The aim of the entrepreneur who eventually operates this venture would be to attract at least two per cent of the active international Wilbur Smith fan club (estimated at more than one million) to visit the house. That would bring an annual minimum of 20,000 foreign tourists to Kabwe, in addition to local tourists. Even if there were no admission charge to the museum, the house would still generate significant revenue from an on-the-premises café and Wilbur Smith books and memorabilia.

Conservatively it can be estimated that 63 foreign visitors a day would visit the Wilbur Smith house. Assuming the tourists spent a modest $10 a day each; the business would generate a daily income of $630 for an annual income of $197,190. This assumes the house would be closed on Sundays. This income would come only from foreigners. Income from Zambians would probably match this, making the proposition extremely attractive to young Zambian entrepreneurs.

The benefits of restoring Wilbur Smith's house into a heritage home open to tourists would go beyond the income earned by the entrepreneur and the employment offered by the business. Guest houses and hotels in Kabwe would also benefit as tourists would need somewhere to sleep. Existing or potential tourist sites would also benefit as the Smith visitors may wish to include them in their itineraries.

There are many other opportunities to be exploited in this way. Certainly Chishimba Falls, Kalambo Falls, and Nkundalila Falls can all be developed with priority given to construction of low cost but comfortable accommodation attractive to local tourists. Concentrating at first on inexpensive accommodation would level the playing field and encourage the participation of Zambian entrepreneurs in the development of these spectacular sights.

Chishimba Falls, comprising the main falls, Kaela Rapids, and Mutumuna Falls, potentially has a very large market for tourists, given its closeness to Tanzania and the Tanzania Zambia railway corridor. Kalambo Falls is just as close with the Kalambo River marking the boundary between Zambia and Tanzania for a short distance.

Kalambo is second only to South Africa's Tugela Falls as the highest uninterrupted falls on the continent. But Kalambo is not just a tourist site, it is also important archaeologically. Carbon dating of tools excavated from Kalambo Gorge suggests human activity there stretching back more than 300,000 years. For both sight-seeing and archaeological reasons therefore Kalambo is a national treasure whose potential must be exploited urgently.

Nkundalila is also an obvious site for development. Thanks to its central location, it does get some visitors from the Copperbelt and Lusaka provinces. These visitors tend to be campers and in the absence of facilities spend little or no money in the community.

All three sites and indeed all potential tourist areas in Zambia also have a huge international market to tap into.

Two examples illustrate the point. According to Statistics Canada, Canadians spent a record $29.5 billion on travel to the top 15 countries in 2013. That represents a huge increase over the $12.8 billion spent in 2010. 2014 and 2015 may well show a decline because of the weaker Canadian dollar which has discouraged travel to the United States, but the figures will still be significant. Indeed the weaker Canadian dollar that discourages travel to the United States may well encourage Canadians to travel to cheaper destinations like Zambia.

The second example is from China.

Germany's largest market research institute, GfK Global, reported on January 14, 2016 that China produced 109 million outbound tourists in 2015. These tourists had a retail spending power of US$229 billion.

Zambia has good relations with both countries and could realistically mount a 'Visit Zambia' campaign directed at the two countries' travelling public. A strategy that targeted five per cent of these tourists for Zambia would not be unrealistic.

Strategic success would thus result in Zambia earning $1.5 billion from Canada and $11 billion from China.

Unlocking Cash for Investment

There are other resources available for Zambian development in addition to the potential revenue from tourism. Zambia has assets that can be liquidated but still continue to perform for the benefit of the nation.

A good example comes from the health sector. Over the past thirty years, it has been fashionable for ailing Zambian political leaders to be sent abroad for treatment. Since the end of apartheid, the favourite destination for Zambia's sick politicians has been South Africa. But whether the political elite have travelled to Europe or within Southern Africa, the cost of medical related travel has been enormous for Zambia. The common excuse advanced for not using Zambian hospitals and health centres is that these institutions are not sufficiently equipped and may not have all the necessary facilities, although they may have excellent doctors.

The money spent on medical-related travel could be saved by establishing a world class hospital in Lusaka that would serve both local and international patients. The current University Teaching Hospital could be sold to an international medical group with a commitment to provision of excellent medical care. It is difficult to suggest a value for the hospital but we can be sure that its location and the solid although sometimes neglected structures would be attractive to many investors.

We can also be guided by the cost of building new hospitals elsewhere in the world in attempting to set a value for the University Teaching Hospital. For example, the 532 bed University of Texas South western William P Clements Jr.

University Hospital which opened on December 06, 2014 cost $800 million to construct. On the other hand the 862 bed New Parkland Memorial Dallas Hospital which opened August 20, 2015 cost $1.3 billion.

The cost per bed for both hospitals was $1.5 million. It is usual to calculate the costs of hospital construction in 'per bed' terms. In this regard the usual cost of an NHS hospital in the United Kingdom is $638,000 a bed. The cost in Bangalore, India is even lower at $30,000 per bed.

On October 02, 2013, the Dangote Foundation began construction of what was then billed "Africa's most ambitious health facilities" in the Northern Nigerian state of Kano. The 1000 bed hospital would cost $12 million. The cost per bed of the hospital would therefore be $12,000.

As illustrated above, the cost per bed varies; but we have enough data to give us an idea of what would be a reasonable price for selling the University Teaching Hospital in Lusaka. But before coming to that, it is worth recalling the reasons advanced by the philanthropically minded Aliko Dangote to build this modern hospital in Nigeria.

Dangote was motivated by a deep seated desire to end medical tourism, which, according to the then Central Bank of Nigeria Governor Sanusi Lamido Sanusi cost the country $480 million a year. According to the Organising Committee of the Nigerian Centenary Charity Ball this figure is an underestimate. The Organising Committee calculated in October 2013 that Nigerians actually spend around N250bn (US$1.6bn) a year on medical treatment abroad.

Zambians should be equally motivated to end the kind of medical tourism that has been so costly to the treasury.

The University Teaching Hospital has approximately 1655 beds and 250 baby cots. Its comparative value however in relation to the Maria Sanusi Dantata hospital in Kano goes beyond the number of beds. The Dangote hospital will be situated at a wing of the Murtala Muhammed Specialist Hospital in Kano whereas the University Teaching Hospital in Lusaka is a standalone complex occupying a huge chunk of land in a prime location. Furthermore the University Teaching Hospital has the following reasonably well equipped departments:

- Department of Anaesthesia
- Department of Internal Medicine
- Department of Obstetrics and Gynaecology
- Department of Paediatrics
- Department of Surgery
- Department of Community Medicine
- Department of Pathology
- Radiology Department
- Physiotherapy Department
- Pharmacy Department
- Blood Bank

The existence of these departments added to the ideal location of the hospital would suggest that the UTH has considerable value.

Bearing all this in mind, the costs of constructing the four hospitals we have looked at are relevant. Thus if Zambia wanted a hospital to the standard of an NHS hospital in the United Kingdom, the cost per bed would be $638,000 less the difference in construction labour costs between the UK and Zambia. Even if we assumed that the cost of construction in Zambia would be half that in the UK, the starting point in attempting to assess the value of the UTH would be around $500 million. (There are many contractors who take the view that construction costs may actually be higher in Zambia)

Let's be conservative however and assume a sale value of only $250 million. If UTH were sold on this basis, some of the proceeds of sale could then be earmarked for construction of two health centres with in patient capacity in each province.

The British born humanitarian architect Cameron Sinclair has developed a method of constructing fully equipped clinics at a cost of $200,000. The figure includes the cost of operating the facility for a year. The analysis here uses the higher figure of $400,000 per health centre because of the requirement of inpatient capacity, assumed at 100.

Bearing this in mind, the $250 million realised from the sale of the University Teaching Hospital would be enough to construct two new health centres in each one of Zambia's ten provinces, create a trust fund for procurement of medicines and equipment not provided for in the national budget, and contribute to investment in the education of doctors, nurses, and other medical personnel. The proposed split would be $8 million; $100 million; and $142 million.

The new owners of the University Teaching Hospital would be obliged, as part of transition arrangements, to care for low income patients pending completion of the new health centres and thereafter to allow a certain number of low income Lusaka residents to be treated without fee.

Unlocking cash tied up in the UTH would allow Zambia a world class hospital able to provide medical attention previously only available abroad; build 20 new medical facilities (collectively with more beds than the UTH) mostly in rural areas; create a trust fund to help guarantee availability of medicines and vital equipment in the new hospitals; and increase investment in the education and training of medical personnel. All this would be done without resorting to international aid.

In the same manner, additional resources could be unlocked for education. For example, the two Kabulonga schools (Gilbert Rennie and Jean Rennie to older readers) could be offered for sale to purchasers keen on establishing first rate secondary schools for boys and girls in Zambia. With the cost of public school education in the United Kingdom becoming prohibitive, there is huge interest in alternative ways of providing this kind of education less expensively. The two Kabulonga schools have ample premises and are located in a prime area of Lusaka and despite neglect over the past forty years they have much to offer by way of solid structures, playing fields, a swimming pool, and a squash court that can be rehabilitated.

Indeed the two schools were run along the lines of English boarding schools until the late 1960s.

It is not necessary for our purposes to determine the precise cash value of the two schools but we can estimate what the schools are likely to fetch. During the debate on academy schools in the United Kingdom in 2006, the British government said some non-academy schools offering a lower quality of education, cost up to £35m or US $54 million.

The cost of the average academy school on the other hand was between £25-30m or between US$ 38.7- 46.4 million. This type of academy school would be built for about 1,300 pupils.

To be competitive and encourage the right buyers, the Kabulonga schools would have to be seen as offering more than an equivalent school in England or indeed South Africa, the other destination for seekers of a relatively inexpensive English public school education.

None of the academy schools discussed has the expansive grounds and potential of the Kabulonga schools. There is however a new school in Zambia that has more expansive grounds than the Kabulonga schools (sitting on more than 100 hectares of land) and offers similar facilities to those enjoyed at the two Kabulonga schools in their heyday.

The socially responsible mining group, First Quantum Minerals Ltd. established this world-class school in north western Zambia as a way of promoting international educational standards in the country.

Trident College opened its doors in January 2014 with a student population of 120. Indicative of international demand for high quality education, even at this early stage, Trident found itself welcoming students from foreign countries such as Kenya and Tanzania. Like the Kabulonga schools of bygone days, Trident College offers its pupils the Cambridge University School Curriculum for both the Ordinary and Advanced Levels. The school aims to be at the cutting edge of providing a holistic international boarding school experience.

In addition to traditional subjects like Physics, Chemistry, Biology, English, Mathematics, Modern Languages, History, and Art, the school also offers Design and Technology, Information and Communication Technology (ICT), and Music.

In due course, the school will increase its student population to 400, the same number as attended Kabulonga Boys School in the 1960s.

Trident College cost $50 million to build. That figure would not be unreasonable as a benchmark in determining the value of each one of the Kabulonga schools. Considering the Kabulonga location, in a well-developed part of Zambia, the two schools could fetch as much as $100 million collectively.

It is proposed that 50 per cent of this money be used for equipping existing schools, given the very large number of schools that are not able to function for want of basic equipment such as desks which can be made at home.

A few years ago I visited a Zambian owned information technology college in Ndola. I was impressed by the orderliness of the establishment and could not help noticing that the college had neat functional desks finished in vinyl. I asked the owner of the college where he had purchased the desks. Had they been imported? I still recall the smile on his face when he triumphantly explained that the desks had been made in the backyard of the premises he operated from, mostly from discarded wood. He did admit that the vinyl itself was imported.

A tender for the construction and installation of desks in schools across the country could be issued. To maximise local content and reduce costs, the vinyl could be dispensed with on this occasion!

The unit cost of constructing desks in North America ranges from $5 to a $100 with desks made in highly automated factories having a lower unit cost than desks made largely by hand. Because of lower labour costs in Zambia, desks made by hand in the country would be much cheaper than desks made by hand in North America.

There are 184 primary schools, 147 secondary schools, and 41 colleges in Zambia. These figures exclude international schools and universities. The pupil population in primary and secondary schools ranges from below 300 to 800. The schools alone would constitute a viable market for local suppliers of desks. The combined number of primary and secondary schools is 331 with an average pupil population of 550. That translates into a total population of 182,000. That is the number of desks to be made and supplied as needed. The value of this business at a cost of $50 per desk is $9.1 million. Most of this money would go to individual desk manufacturers in rural or semi-urban areas, because most schools are in these areas. The recipients of this cash would probably be peasant farmers in their other lives, and would almost certainly use part of this income to enhance their farming capacity.

All this would be done inexpensively with the cost of making desks barely making a dent in the sale price of the Kabulonga schools, as there would still be $40.9 million left over from the money earmarked for school equipment. This money could be spent on necessities like science laboratory equipment. The remaining $50 million should be put into a trust fund to guarantee future equipment purchases and training of teachers not provided for in the national budget.

Ending Residential Squalor

Kanyama Township is an entirely unplanned habitat south of Lusaka. For the most part the area has no running water and exhibits all the characteristics of a slum neglected by officialdom. Since the late 1970s Kanyama has been the victim of flooding in each year that Zambia has had anything resembling above normal rainfall. The first recorded serious deluge occurred in 1978. Times were different then and the country was more responsive to suffering than it perhaps is now. Businesspeople and ordinary men and women were joined by the international community in raising money for what came to be known as the Kanyama Disaster Fund. The purpose of the fund was to help accommodate, feed and otherwise help the victims of the disaster.

Since it was clear from the start that the flooding could have been avoided had the Lusaka City Council constructed an appropriate drainage system, the hope was that drainage infrastructure would now be put in place to avoid similar disasters in the future.

Sadly that did not happen. There was no public explanation either of how the huge amount of money raised was used by the local authority. Virtually each rainy season brings flooding to Kanyama, with the deluge of 1978 proportions being repeated frequently in the recent past. This was certainly the case during the 2009/2010 rainy season which caused widespread flooding.

The *Post* newspaper edition of March 10, 2010 described the flooding as a 'death trap'. The newspaper had reason to do so. At least 12 children in the area were reported to have died in the floods. During the week that *the Post* article was written, the government and the Zambia Red Cross Society relocated over 800 people to the Lusaka Independence Stadium where they were obliged to sleep in tents, use mobile toilets, and prepare food in communal kitchens. That population of internal refugees included 200 children of school age. One of the children, 14 year-old Memory Phiri, explained that she had been unable to attend school since her house was submerged by the floods, a month earlier.

This misery could have been avoided had the local authority built the needed drainage infrastructure way back in 1978 or even a little later. The residents of Kanyama continue to suffer from preventable diseases brought on by unsanitary conditions. These diseases of course multiply during the hot rainy season when floods are likely to occur.

The most important resource in building a drainage system is labour. In addition, piping, stone, sand, cement, and excavation equipment are also required. All these are available in Zambia. Why then has the Kanyama drainage system not been built, as required by Zambian town and country planning law? Given the regularity of the flooding and its consequent predictability, why are the authorities always taken by surprise when floods occur? There has been no lack of opportunity for both levels of government to end Kanyama's vulnerability to flooding.

This vulnerability is well known. What is less publicised is the fact that a Zambian controlled firm of architects and property developers in South Africa did offer to convert Kanyama into a properly serviced residential area with proper drainage. When the offer was initially made, the Zambian government, while appreciating the benefits of such a project, expressed concerned that if the offer was accepted, the Opposition, which controlled local government, might get too much credit for the improvement in the standard of living for Kanyama residents.

Subsequently, President Mwanawasa was convinced that rebuilding shanty towns as outlined by the South African firm would be a good thing for the country. He therefore directed the firm to send the plans to him for action. The plans were sent but the President claimed not to have received them. The head of state then suggested that perhaps the project documentation could be handed to the Zambian mission in Pretoria and marked for the attention of the first lady. Mr Mwanawasa was convinced that this way the documentation would reach him. He was right. The documents were sent promptly to State House and Differ Mulimba, the president's special assistant, confirmed receipt of the plans.

Confirmation of receipt of the documents was the only good news the property developers heard from the Zambian state. No further action was taken by the government.

Michael Sata as leader of the opposition was quick to point out the government's shortcomings in addressing Kanyama's issues. In February 2010, he warned the government that its poor response to the floods could lead to a revolution. In an interview with *the Post* newspaper he predicted that "the blood of the flood victims shall forever haunt" the ruling party, directing his remarks specifically at Vice-President George

Kunda. The Vice President in Zambia heads the country's emergency response system.

How easily political allegiances change! In the same interview Sata praised the UPND leader Hakainde Hichilema and the PF Vice President, Guy Scott for showing leadership by visiting the areas affected by the floods. At that time there was an electoral pact between Sata's party and Mr. Hichilema's United Party for National Development.

Michael Sata and Hakainde Hichilema. A short lived alliance

Referring specifically to his plan for areas like Kanyama, Sata promised that when in government his team "will walk with you in times of trouble and not fly over your heads at a high cost that would have saved dozens of lives and unblocked the storm drains and culverts."

He continued:

How many more must die before we say enough is enough? When you wake up tomorrow or next week, ask not whom the bell of failure tolls for… it tolls for [President] Banda and the MMD, their time is up. You need a leadership which is on the ground not in the air; you need the PF-UPND pact, Sata and HH because we walk the walk and talk the talk.

What a pity that President Sata never revived the plan by the Zambian owned South African firm to modernise Kanyama.

Another candidate for upgrading would be the less underprivileged but not ideal Kalingalinga settlement which is located in a prime area of Lusaka between the Kabulonga residential area and the Great East Road leading to the international airport. Given its location and the exceptionally high demand for good residential property in Lusaka, it would not be difficult to lease the entire settlement to property developers.

The purpose of the development would be the creation of a modern residential area with proper sewage and drainage systems and recreational facilities. In order to achieve this dream a number of existing structures would of course have to be erased. These structures do however have a value to the current occupants. For this reason the agreement allowing property developers to acquire Kalingalinga would include provision for payment of fair compensation to people losing their homes. With this compensation the previously cash strapped residents of Kalingalinga would have more choices; they could use the money to settle farther away from urban Lusaka and invest in agriculture, or they could find other accommodation in Lusaka, or indeed invest in the development corporation that now owned the township.

A good model for taking over Kalingalinga would be one that encouraged residents to acquire shares in the development company.

Some residents would of course choose to be bought out but others may be interested in owning shares with a real market value. The opportunity to buy shares in the new company should be open both to those deciding to stay in the new Kalingalinga as well as those deciding to leave.

Encouraging this kind of ownership would also release hundreds of millions of Kwacha believed to be in mattresses in settlements like Kalingalinga, into the formal sector of the economy.

A Sustainable Environment for Growth

President Sata missed the opportunity to adopt policies likely to lead to robust economic growth and empowerment of ordinary Zambians. Thanks to the reforms of the early 1990s, Mr. Sata presided over a growing economy with increased economic activity and consequent rise in demand for virtually all products. Although this was generally beneficial, the new Zambian economy also compounded environmental challenges such as deforestation.

Whether or not we blame government policy for deforestation or take the view that poverty or the poor are to blame, it is undeniable that harvesting of trees for charcoal production is a main cause of forest loss. It is therefore important that in implementing growth-oriented policies, the government encourages the use of appropriate technology and effectively discourages deforestation.

Too many Zambians rely on charcoal for basic energy and this demand leads to destruction of trees at an unsustainable rate. It need not be that way. Zambians can get alternative energy for household purposes such as cooking that is less damaging to the environment. There is for example a solar cooker that can be built easily and cheaply and adopted as the main source of energy for households currently dependent on charcoal.

The cooker is made primarily from windscreen shade, and has been tested successfully around the world. The other pieces of equipment needed to make the cooker are a grill, black pot, bucket and a plastic bag. Individuals who have tried to make the cooker at home in North America have been able to do so for $10! As long as the cooker is pointed toward the sun it can get very hot, reaching a temperature of 350 degrees!

This cooker is more efficient than the traditional Zambian brazier. Serious consideration should therefore be given to encouraging this as the main source of energy in homes currently using the brazier.

At the same time as solar energy is encouraged as a way of reducing dependency on charcoal, Zambia should seriously turn its attention to reforestation. Reforestation is crucial in the effort to improve the quality of Zambian life; as the forests soak up pollution and dust from the air, rebuild natural habitats and ecosystems, and reduce the negative impact of global warming.

There is another advantage of reforestation for Zambia - it creates an opportunity for large scale employment as thousands of people would be required to cover deforested areas across the country with new trees. President Sata recognised this. In December 2012 he launched an ambitious nationwide tree-planting programme that would see 25 million trees planted throughout Zambia.

Speaking at the launch of the programme at Kanakantapa in Chongwe district, the president opined that with proper management the forestry sector could help raise Zambian prosperity significantly. He further saw reforestation as a way of combating climate change because:

> Forests not only alleviate poverty by sustaining food and productive eco-system for agriculture and water development but also assist in the reduction of greenhouse gases which have led to global warming, resulting in climate change.

This was reassuring given the rate of deforestation in Zambia. According to Doreen Nawa, a development practitioner, an area of forest the size of a football pitch is cut down every 10 minutes for agricultural purposes, charcoal production and construction. That translates into 300,000 hectares of forest being lost every year due to deforestation, concludes Nawa who has analysed the statistics in this sector.

Information is scanty on how President Sata's initiative has fared. We do know however that a non-profit organisation called Greepop, active mostly in the Livingstone area, has planted roughly 5000 trees a year since 2013.

At the other end of the country, in Chingola, a mining company in the private sector has also committed to planting 100,000 trees. 2,350 trees were planted in 2015, making a total of 7,000 trees planted since 2014 by Konkola Copper Mines.

Sata took the initiative to place tree planting on the development agenda. It appears however that the Zambian public service has not been diligent in implementing the initiative. Once again the Zambian people were ready to move forward but their institutions of government let them down.

It's about the People

Government institutions need to recognise Zambians as a people with the ingenuity to move their economy forward. Real economic development and prosperity can only come from Zambians, regardless of ethnicity, first language, gender, skin colour or birth circumstance. With the kinds of policies advocated in this book, Zambians do not need coercion to advance their country. They only need reaffirmation of their freedom and integrity to tap into their legendary creativity for the good of their country. Thus far the free market system so bravely reintroduced in the early 1990s has been used largely for the benefit of foreigners and Zambians chosen (or at least tolerated) for success by the regime. The commitment to merit has not been evident, and consequently innovative Zambians unknown to the political elite have been denied the opportunity to use their innovation for the good of the country.

It is time to allow an economy for the people to emerge, as only when ordinary people feel connected to the formal economy and believe in the institutions of government, will wide spread prosperity be possible.

Government's primary role in creating the new Zambia is to institute the necessary policy framework and commit to serving their nationals without discrimination. The Zambian people will do the rest.

CHAPTER FOURTEEN

Sata's Achievements

Michael Sata's acerbic tongue and undiplomatic behaviour have left indelible impressions on many political commentators. His failure on account of illness to tackle corruption has already been alluded to as has the missed opportunity to create a new democratic economy for Zambia.

Despite all this however, the Sata presidency did make notable progress in at least three areas. Firstly, Sata asserted Zambian sovereignty by sending a clear signal that Zambians were not to be treated as second class citizens in their land. Secondly, Sata placed infrastructure expansion on the Zambian development agenda. Thirdly, Sata was aggressive in promoting gender equality and gave women a practical voice in the management of state affairs.

Sata believed in Zambian sovereignty and dignity as his relationship with Chinese investors in the country demonstrates.

The political party formed by Michael Sata in 2001 was electorally insignificant until Sata utilized his old trade union activist skills and made himself the champion of workers employed by Chinese companies. The Chinese who quickly established a reputation for poor working conditions were also notorious for safety regulation breaches in the mines they operated. Chinese companies generally found Zambian employment and safety standards cumbersome.

In late October 2010 Chinese managers of a coal mining company in southern Zambia responded to a protest against poor pay and conditions by opening fire. 13 Zambian workers were wounded as a result of the shooting.

Sata seized this moment. He attacked the government of Rupiah Banda which he accused of indifference to the plight of Zambian workers. He added that the government had been "heavily corrupted by the Chinese for the 2011 elections…"

It did not help matters that on April 04, 2011 government prosecutors announced their decision not to prosecute the Chinese supervisors who had carried out the shootings.

Sata pledged to protect 'innocent' Zambian workers against Chinese investors whom he derogatorily referred to as 'infesters.' His criticism of the Chinese was so severe that the latter departed from their practice of not commenting on party politics in Zambia by declaring that if Sata won the 2011 elections, they would consider taking their investments out of the country.

It has been suggested that the Chinese believed doing so would shut down the copper mining industry on which Zambia depended for foreign exchange earnings. More importantly the Chinese reportedly believed this would lead to massive redundancies. They may have exaggerated their own importance in this regard. Canadian, Swiss and Indian mining companies are much larger players in the Zambian copper mining industry than the Chinese are.

In any event the Chinese threat did nothing to weaken Sata. The public handed him a relatively easy victory in the 2011 presidential election. In a sign that the recalcitrant foreigners had lost this particular battle, China was among the first countries to send a delegation to congratulate and honour the new Zambian head of state. There was no more talk of divesting from Zambia.

While President Sata was gracious in victory, he did not miss the opportunity to tell the Chinese they could stay only on condition that they respected Zambians and the law of the land.

The Chinese appeared to understand that the days of treating Zambian workers as second class citizens in their own land were over. A high-profile visit was arranged to China in 2013 to afford Sata an opportunity to meet President Xi Jinping and other high-ranking Chinese officials. According to the journal *African Business* there had been "a 'night of the long knives' during which errant Chinese managers and their supervisors in Africa were hauled over the coals, and general oversight on how the Chinese behaved in Africa was sharpened up."

Sata had always been irritated by what he saw as kowtowing to foreigners by his predecessor, Rupiah Banda. He took the opportunity in this case to show the Chinese and anyone else who cared to take notice that he was not prepared to tolerate ill treatment of his people even by investors. Anyone wanting to do business in Zambia had to respect Zambians. The country was sovereign and her people were entitled to live in dignity regardless of who they worked for.

No Development without Infrastructure

The president was concerned that almost five decades after attaining statehood Zambia did not have an infrastructure that connected all its parts. During the 2006 election campaign Sata promised to build a hospital every 120 kilometers between populated areas, if elected. He also promised secondary schools in every location with a significant population. Many, like the late Professor Alfred Chanda, Chair of Transparency International Zambia, considered these promises unrealistic. And yet real progress was made. Thus by April 2014 the Sata government had commissioned the Lufwanyama Hospital constructed at a cost of $2.1m. At the official opening of the hospital, Chitalu Chilufya, the Deputy Minister of Health described the occasion as 'yet another milestone towards the attainment of equity' in health care access.

The Deputy Minister also noted that prior to the construction of the hospital patients in the area were referred to Kitwe Central Hospital which was 80 kilometres away from Lufwanyama.

So, Sata's promise in 2006 that no one should travel more than 120 kilometres for hospital treatment may not have been that unrealistic after all. Although in office for only three years, Sata may well be remembered as the Infrastructure President. Under his leadership the Zambian government initiated many road development projects, including the Link Zambia 8000 whose aim was to rehabilitate existing roads and create new roads across the country. Link Zambia 8000 particularly benefitted rural areas which in the past often felt left out of development opportunities. Pave Zambia 2000 and L200 road projects on the other hand focused on the rehabilitation of roads in Lusaka. (Not all these initiatives were entirely new as some of them were a continuation of the work commenced by President Rupiah Banda.)

Kitwe-Chingola Road

In initiating the Link Zambia 8000 programme in 2012 Sata's declared intent was to turn land locked Zambia into 'land-linked Zambia.' The objective here was not only to significantly increase connectivity and accessibility but also to lower transportation costs.

By the time of his death nearly 2,000 kilometres of road at a total cost of $100m was under construction. Four months after Sata's death (on March 04, 2015) the cabinet minister responsible for roads told parliament that as of December 31, 2014; 2,616 km had been procured out of which 406.09 km had been surfaced and opened to traffic while other roads were 'at different levels of completion.' Had Sata been alive he would have relished the next statement from the minister:

> Furthermore the programme, since its inception, has created over 18,000 jobs in the road construction industry. Under this programme, the road links from Copperbelt to North Western Provinces will be upgraded to a dual carriageway...

The construction of roads in rural areas was noticed and appreciated by local residents. When Sata died it was his effort in expanding Zambia's physical infrastructure that most mourners recalled with fondness. This was certainly the case when the district commissioner for Isoka, Joe Siwila, was interviewed in the aftermath of the president's death. According to the local official Isoka residents were 'saddened by President Sata's death and will always be grateful to him for taking development to the area.' (*Zambia Daily Mail November 03, 2014*)

Among other developments Siwila cited the construction of Michael Chilufya Sata Girls Secondary School, the paving of township roads and improvement of water supply and sanitation as evidence of Sata's concern for ordinary citizens. In Mr. Siwila's words, Sata 'had a heart for the poor.'

Siwila further expressed the hope that Zambia's next leader would be as active as Sata had been in infrastructure development. Indeed many commentators acknowledge that because of the expectations created by Michael Sata it will be very difficult for future presidents to ignore infrastructure development.

Neither was Sata's vision confined to road construction. He saw a link between good roads on the one hand and primary health care and education on the other. He paid attention to the health and education sectors too.

The Sata government commissioned four district hospitals in Chadiza, Chiengi, Nakonde and Shangombo, in addition to Lufwanyama. At the time of his death 30 district hospitals were under construction in different parts of Zambia. Plans were also underway to construct an additional eight district hospitals in Mafinga, Ikelenge, Nalolo, Limulunga, Vubwi, Mansa, Mufulira and Chilubi by the end of 2014.

Neither did construction of new hospitals come at the expense of refurbishing existing ones. The Sata government also procured and installed modern and specialised medical equipment at existing hospitals like the University Teaching Hospital in Lusaka, Kitwe and Ndola Central hospitals, and the Livingstone General Hospital.

In addition to building district hospitals, President Sata's government also embarked upon an ambitious project to construct 650 health posts across the country. The cost of the project stood at $55 million with $50 million of that being in the form of an Indian government concessionary loan.

Sensibly, the Sata government carried out a rigorous procurement process based on international best practices to identify contractors to build the health posts. The 650 health posts were split into three lots in order to minimize the risk that may result from awarding the entire project to one contractor. Thus Central, Copperbelt, and Eastern provinces constituted the first lot. Northwest, Muchinga, and Luapula provinces made up the second lot, with Western, Southern, and Lusaka provinces constituting the third lot. The respective amounts allocated to the lots were $19.46 million, $18.1 million, and $18.3 million respectively.

In January 2016, the Zambian government expressed confidence that the health posts would be completed by April 2016. The Deputy Minister for Health, Chitalu Chilufya told the Times of Zambia on January 04, 2016 that the government was committed to ensuring that health posts were completed and handed over to the public by April.

This timeline was unrealistic and by May 13, 2016 President Lungu could only announce that out of the 650 health posts being constructed across the country, 170 were operational and offering 'great health services to the people.' On the hospital front, the president reported that his government had constructed 39 district hospitals five of which were operational. (*Lusaka Times*)

Education Infrastructure

The importance of expanding the education infrastructure was recognised by the MMD government especially under the leadership of Rupiah Banda. This helped the Sata administration to boast 83 schools under construction during its first year in office.

From the very start of his administration Sata made it clear he was going to expand the education sector not only by building more schools but also by constructing new universities.

Within 18 months of taking office, Education Minister John Phiri was telling the nation that his government would open a new university in each one of Zambia's ten provinces. His justification was that the existing universities did not have the capacity to absorb all the young people from secondary schools wishing to pursue higher education.

In addition to building the new universities the Sata government also pledged to rehabilitate the country's three publically funded universities although the $60 million needed for the exercise was not allocated until 2015.

One of the new universities was completed in late 2015. Robert Kapasa Makasa University of Science and Technology is a well-designed university occupying a lovely spot of northern Zambia. Remarkably, very little was said about how this university would be equipped and managed during the period of construction.

Robert Makasa University under construction

It was not until November 2015 that the government directed the University of Zambia to 'open Robert Kapasa Makasa University as soon as possible and run it.'

Robert Makasa University

The directive raised eye brows in academic circles outside the University of Zambia, given UNZA's own management history. The reputation that the University of Zambia enjoyed until the mid-1980s has all but disappeared. Gone are the days when graduates of UNZA could easily compete for post graduate places at universities like Oxford, Cambridge, Harvard, and Yale.

During the graduation ceremony of December 2013, the University of Zambia's own chancellor bemoaned his institution's poor showing on the Webometrics ranking of universities. According to that ranking UNZA came 66th in Africa and 3,970[th] in the world. The world ranking for 2016 was 4,126[th]. There is no polite way of describing this kind of ranking which surely emanates from neglect and poor management. One consequence of this poor performance is that the University of Oxford, home of the Rhodes Trust, no longer recognizes degrees from the University of Zambia.

By asking the poorly managed University of Zambia to manage the new Robert Kapasa Makasa University the Zambian government condemned the new institution to mediocrity even before it was born. Robert Kapasa Makasa University of Science and Technology presents an opportunity to depart from institutional mediocrity. The Zambian government should have sought a partnership for Robert Kapasa Makasa University with an international university of repute. One such university would be Waterloo in Ontario, Canada.

The University of Waterloo was launched in 1957 by a group of industrialists whose dream was to change the world through innovation and research. Waterloo is now an internationally recognized leader in entrepreneurship and innovation.

Robert Kapasa Makasa University could learn a great deal from Waterloo whose mission's core is teaching and research excellence. It is no wonder that despite its youth, the university has (at the time of writing) been ranked Canada's most innovative university for the 23rd consecutive year. *Maclean's* magazine has also ranked Waterloo as Canada's best overall university for 19 of the last 23 years.

Waterloo's reputation is not limited to Canada. The Times Higher Education Rankings place Waterloo at No. 179 for 2015-2016. (The California Institute of Technology and Oxford University take the first two spots.)

Unlike Nigeria's Ibadan, Kenya's Nairobi, and Uganda's Makerere, the University of Zambia does not feature at all on the Times Higher Education World University Rankings whose performance tables judge world class universities across their entire core missions of teaching, research, knowledge transfer and international outlook.

A request for partnership would not be too surprising to Waterloo because it already describes itself as being 'at the hub of a growing network of global partnerships.' Waterloo would see an association with RKM as an opportunity to shape the future by building bridges with industry and between disciplines, institutions and communities. The reader will not be too surprised to learn that international students make up 14 per cent of Waterloo's population. The female to male ratio at 45:55 is quite healthy for a science and technology university. At 24:2 the student to staff ratio is equally impressive.

Closing the Gender Gap

Michael Sata may never have crafted a policy paper on governance and gender equality but he understood instinctively that a central element of good governance was the responsiveness of policies and public institutions to the needs of all citizens including women. He knew that policies and institutions must represent the interests of both genders and promote equal access to resources.

President Sata was also aware that women were generally more disadvantaged than men. This was particularly true with rural women engaged in small scale farming. According to the United Nations Entity for Gender Equality and the Empowerment of Women, while extreme poverty in Zambia stands at 42 per cent, the figure for rural dwellers is 58 per cent. The populist Mr. Sata would instinctively have wanted to address this imbalance. It is not surprising that he found what came to be known as the Zambia Social Cash Transfer Programme of great interest. Once the programme was up and running, most beneficiaries turned out to be women.

To be clear, the Sata government was not the first to consider cash support for the country's most vulnerable citizens. As the German sociologist, Daniel Kumitz has observed, the first pilot was done in 2003 in Kalomo, and was meant to provide relief from food insecurity among AIDS affected households by providing a second meal each day. The number of households benefitting from the programme was 159. Each household received $7 representing $31.8 in purchasing power at that time.

In 2006 the Mwanawasa government pledged support but not much came out of that pledge because of the then finance minister's opposition to the plan. After Mwanawasa's death, the new president, Rupiah Banda, included the Social Cash Transfer Programme in the sixth National Development Plan with modest target numbers.

In 2011, the newly elected President Sata promised to scale up the programme in the context of a more comprehensive policy.

At the opening of the fourth session of the national assembly in September 2014, the Sata government announced a 700 per cent increase in the allocation to the Social Cash Transfer Programme. As a result the number of beneficiary households increased to 145,000 compared to 63,000 the previous year. President Sata further promised a National Social Protection Bill to be tabled before parliament. The purpose of the bill would be to provide a framework for comprehensive social security for citizens.

On March 07, 2016 Professor Evance Kalula, the Zambian born Rhodes Scholar and labour law professor at Cape Town University produced the first draft of the Legal Framework for Social Protection in Zambia. He was ably assisted in this enterprise by two young Zambian students, Kangwa-Musole George Chisanga and Chanda Chungu.

The stated objectives of the proposed law are the alleviation of poverty for the extremely vulnerable; the assurance of a livelihood for employees with limited or no capacity to work; and also the assurance of the livelihood of surviving family members in the event of a breadwinner dying.

The draft Legal Framework for Social Protection in Zambia adopts an approach to reducing poverty and promoting economic growth that stresses the importance of community engagement with the public institutions that make decisions that affect the socio economic well-being of citizens.

Sata saw good governance as essential to the approach adopted in the Framework. While in opposition he repeatedly talked about the importance of public institutions being efficient, transparent, and accountable. In office he clearly saw the value of making the processes of governance inclusive and participatory.

This is the context to Sata's clear commitment to gender equality which he saw as a means for achieving development. He wanted women to have a stronger voice in decision making.

Reference has already been made to President Sata's decision to choose Madam Justice Lombe Chibesakunda, Zambia's first female lawyer, as acting Chief Justice. As pointed out earlier Madam Justice Chibesakunda has an impressive résumé. She was called to the Bar at Gray's Inn in 1969. She then served as a Zambian state advocate for six years before trying her hand at private practice for a year. She went back to the public sector in 1973 to serve as Solicitor General, Deputy Minister of Legal Affairs, and Member of Parliament for the Lusaka constituency of Matero. In addition to these accomplishments she also served as Ambassador to Japan and High Commissioner to the United Kingdom.

Her foray into the judiciary started with an appointment as Chair of the Industrial Relations Court. She ended up as a Supreme Court judge. It was from these ranks that Michael Chilufya Sata selected her for the Chief Justice position. Her tenure may have been turbulent but it also inspired many young women who now saw that they could participate in the affairs of the nation at very high levels. The expectation of gender equality in the judiciary was cemented when another woman was appointed to succeed Chibesakunda.

Within six months of assuming office, Sata appointed 39 year old Stella Libongani as the top law enforcement officer in the country, making her the first woman and the youngest person to hold that office in Zambia's history. This was the second time Ms. Libongani had made history. On October 03, 2011 she became the first woman to be appointed Deputy Inspector General of Police.

The international community took notice. There was certainly excitement in the Southern African Development Community whose Protocol on Gender and Development calls on states to take appropriate measures to ensure women are equally represented in decision making positions in all sectors. At home the appointment was seen as yet another sign of the Sata government's commitment to the elevation of women to significant decision making positions.

These appointments were not afterthoughts. Sata had always wanted to increase the participation of women in the management of Zambian affairs. When he formed his then opposition Patriotic Front party, he insisted that a woman, Inonge Mutukwa Wina, be the non-executive head of the organization. Wina was certainly qualified for the position. She holds a diploma in social work from Santa Monica City College in Los Angeles and a Bachelor of Arts degree from the University of Zambia. Mrs. Wina's involvement in community work goes back to the early 1970s when she volunteered as advisor to a number of women's movements. She also has served as president of the Young Women's Christian Association, where she is remembered for championing human rights for women. It was this work that led to the establishment of the Victim Support Unit under the Zambia Police Service.

In 1996, she was elected National Chairperson of the umbrella non-governmental organization group, the NGO Coordinating Council of Zambia.

In addition to all this, Wina also served as director on a number of boards in the public sector including the Zambia Council of Social Services, the University Teaching Hospital, and the University of Zambia Council. In making her chairperson of the Patriotic Front party, Sata chose well.

A week after being sworn in as president, Michael Sata appointed another woman, Rosewin Wandi, as Director-General of the Anti-Corruption Commission, the lead institution in the fight against corruption in Zambia. Just as in Wina's case, this was not a token or symbolic appointment. Mrs. Wandi came with impressive credentials. She had worked at the Anti-Corruption Commission for more than 25 years where she rose through the ranks to now assume the top position.

A month after Mrs. Wandi's appointment Sata appointed six women as police heads of six of Zambia's ten provinces. Thus Eastern, Lusaka, Northern, Southern, Copperbelt, and Luapula provinces found themselves with females at the top of their police structures.

One of the appointees was Brenda Muntemba who was given the task of commanding the Southern Province.

Brenda Muntemba is the daughter of Bradley and Hillary Muntemba. Her late father had served as commanding officer for the Central province. Brenda's mother Hillary had served on two national constitutional review commissions.

Brenda herself was influenced by her father in joining the police service although she did not do so until a year after his death when she was 26. By all accounts Brenda was an able student. She attended the University of Zambia where she read French and Economics from 1988 to 1992. After obtaining her degree she taught French at Alliance Francaise in addition to her regular secondary school teaching responsibilities. Not content with just a bachelor's degree Brenda enrolled for a Master's Degree in French and English and qualified as an interpreter after a two-year stint in France. This was clearly a meritorious appointment which the head of state had thought about carefully.

When Sata died the country remembered his commitment to gender equality as fondly as it remembered his commitment to expanding national infrastructure. *The Zambia Daily Mail* edition of November 03, 2014 recalled that while successive governments had tried to elevate women, it was Sata who had taken the necessary action. As the Zambia National Women's Lobby remembered, it was Sata who took concrete steps to bridge the gender gap. The Lobby further noted that 40 per cent of the judicial branch of government's decision makers was now female.

Equally important President Sata took steps to ensure that gender equality was constantly on Zambia's development agenda by upgrading the Gender Division Department into a Full-fledged ministry, known as the Ministry of Gender and Child Development.

Inonge Wina, Zambia's first female vice president

Surviving The Cobra's Bite

The period preceding Michael Chilufya Sata's election as president witnessed a relentless propaganda assault on the future president and his party. The effort was led by Chanda Chimba 111 a pro government journalist. In his documentaries under the theme *Stand Up for Zambia*, Chimba predicted that a Sata presidency would convert Zambia into a police state where citizens and foreigners alike would routinely be picked up at night and imprisoned or deported without due process. In this world, freedom of speech would cease to exist and civil war would be all but certain. Chimba used the state media to propagate his fearful message with the active encouragement of the government.

Some of the predictions appear absurd today but back in 2010 and 2011 the government of the day had real fears that Sata would reverse the economic and political gains of the 1990s and effectively reintroduce a Kaunda style one party state. Sata's closeness to the former dictator did not help matters in this regard.

Zambian democracy was however too entrenched for Sata or anyone else to turn back the clock. Nonetheless it did appear on occasion that the new government was intent on punishing political enemies. Because of the entrenchment of Zambian democracy harassment of political foes was achieved through the use of regular legal procedures, not the notorious *Preservation of Public Security Regulations* which only come into play when a state of emergency has been declared.

For example, on November 06, 2013 *the Lusaka Times* reported that the Zambia National Broadcasting Corporation had sued Chanda Chimba in the amount of $50,000 as reimbursement for monies paid in defamation lawsuits as a result of airing documentaries by Chanda during the anti Sata media campaign. The fact of the matter is ZNBC encouraged Chanda Chimba 111 to do these documentaries as did the government of the day.

Chimba's woes went beyond potential civil liability. On May 03, 2016 the Lusaka Magistrates Court found the affable Ronnie Shikapwasha who had served as minister of information in the Banda government as well as Sam Phiri the former permanent secretary for information in the same government with a case to answer in connection with two counts of abuse of authority with respect to the publication of the Stand Up for Zambia television documentary. The third person found with a case to answer was the freelance journalist Chanda Chimba. It was reported on November 30, 2016 that Shikapwasha and Phiri were acquitted of the offence of abuse of office. Unfortunately, Chimba was sentenced to three years in prison for unlawful printing and publishing as well as possession of property suspected of being proceeds of crime.

Sata was not a vindictive man and it is unlikely that he ordered the unnecessary prosecution of Chanda Chimba.

There were however people within the Sata administration who were both small minded and vindictive enough to support the prosecution of Chimba on charges that at worst made him guilty of defaming Sata and the PF.

Clearly Mr. Chimba's efforts came to nothing since the country still voted for Sata. If Chimba had committed a crime, that crime was victimless. Why then would the authorities waste precious time and money pursuing Chimba for allegedly committing a victimless crime when Zambian prosecutors always complain about lack of resources? Surely there were more pressing cases to be pursued by Zambian prosecutors in late 2012 when the decision to charge Chimba was taken.

This is an example of what some critics of Sata's rule have described as occasional crackdowns on the opposition. These excesses did not however turn Zambia into a dictatorship under Michael Sata. Pointedly, Sata did not follow Kaunda's example of declaring a state of emergency that would have given him the power to imprison political opponents at will and limit other freedoms in the constitution. Nonetheless excesses such as the unnecessary harassment of Chanda Chimba 111 and Ronnie Shikapwasha did tarnish the country's reputation.

On the economic front, Sata's government was profligate and introduced ill-conceived laws whose effect was to alarm investors. Sata's brief rule saw a 45% surge in public wages. His Minister of Finance introduced statutory instruments in 2012 that were generally interpreted by the investor community as marking the beginning of foreign exchange controls, something the country had abandoned in 1992. Statutory Instrument 33 prohibited the quoting, paying, demanding, or receiving foreign currency as legal tender for goods, services and other domestic transactions. Statutory Instrument 55 on the other hand empowered the central bank to monitor capital inflows and outflows and other international transactions.

The hastily crafted law did not in fact reintroduce exchange control. A careful reading of Statutory Instrument 33 reveals that its intent was to reinforce the rights of parties wishing to transact in local currency. In other words a party could not be compelled to quote or otherwise transact in foreign currency for domestic transactions. This was certainly the view taken by a prominent silk.

The two statutory instruments were so difficult to understand and implement that the same minister who had introduced them announced their revocation on March 21, 2014. This was yet another example of how far Zambia had moved as a democratic country committed to free enterprise. The two statutory instruments were simply not viable in 2014.

The country's institutions also proved strong enough to withstand turbulence in the ruling party in the aftermath of President Sata's death. The succession issues have already been referred to. Suffice it to say here that the country's vice president, Guy Scott, was constitutionally barred from serving as a substantive chief executive officer for the country. Some commentators went so far as to opine that Mr. Scott could not even serve as interim president. There was concern therefore that there would be a power vacuum when Sata died. At the time of Sata's death Edgar Lungu was acting president. Against the advice of some hardliners in the PF, Lungu did the right thing and surrendered power to Guy Scott who served as acting president until a presidential by election was held. Despite the ambiguity concerning Mr. Scott's status and the factionalism in the ruling party, the constitution prevailed and Zambia held a peaceful presidential poll that saw Edgar Lungu propelled into the presidency.

Lungu went out of his way to assure the public that he was going to be guided by the Sata legacy even as he moved to undo some of Sata's more business unfriendly policies.

In April 2015 Lungu's government announced plans to slash royalty taxes payable by mining companies, abandoning the Sata inspired fiscal regime that the industry had warned threatened thousands of jobs. That regime had eliminated corporate tax on mining companies and raised royalty tax to 20 per cent in opencast mines and 8 per cent in underground operations. This tax was payable whether or not the company made a profit.

Under the Lungu plan income tax would return to 30 percent and royalties would be a uniform 9 percent. A 15 percent variable profit tax was also proposed. Two months earlier the conciliatory Mr. Lungu had loosened tax regulations for exporters including mining companies, making it easier for them to get value-added tax refunds.

In the longer run it appears Mr. Sata's interventionist policies have not been as deleterious to the country as feared. Zambia does appear to be on the way to retrieving its reputation as an investor friendly country. On December 02, 2015 the governor of the Zambian central bank announced that the country's net foreign direct investment inflows had risen from US$1.7 billion in 2013 to US$3.2 billion in 2014. He was quoting the 2015 Foreign Private and Investor Perceptions Survey.

It does appear that the Cobra was not as venomous as feared.

Index

A

African Americans, 158, 160

African Development Bank, 22, 184

African Farming Improvement Funds Act, 136

African Union, 132, 144

Agenda for Zambia, 29

Anglo American Corporation, 121

Anti-Corruption Commission, 131, 155, 237

Avondale Housing Estates Limited, 131

B

Bank of Zambia, 91, 97, 126, 185

Bemba, 30, 46, 66, 70, 71, 89

Banda, Rupiah, 23, 24, 29, 79, 90, 97, 106, 132, 138, 150, 151, 152, 153, 224, 225, 226, 229, 234

British Foreign Office, 48

Burgess, Guy, 48, 49

Bussières, Jacques, 185

C

Canada, 43, 44, 116, 117, 150, 156, 201, 205, 232, 233

Cape Town University, 235

Carlington Sales Company, 116, 117

Central Intelligence Agency, 49

Chali, Justice Isaac, 62, 63

Changala, Brebner, 62, 63, 64

Chartered Association of Certified Accountants, 110

Chikwanda, Alexander Bwalya, 58, 66

Chiluba, Frederick, xi, xii, xiii, 21, 64, 78, 79, 103, 105, 107, 114, 115, 116, 117, 118, 132, 133, 171, 172, 173

Chingola, 195, 220

Chinsali, 104, 108

Chipimo Jr, Elias, 64

Chona Commission, 39, 41

Chona, Mainza, 39

Chrysler Assembly Plant, Belvidere, Illinois, 192

City Parking Solutions, 188

Civic Society for Poverty Reduction, 86

Clayton, Susan Margaret, 22, 47

Cobra, 105, 168, 244

Commonwealth Development Corporation, 34

Copperbelt, 30, 34, 46, 62, 74, 76, 78, 109, 129, 172, 179, 182, 183, 205, 227, 229, 238

Copperbelt Province, 30, 34, 76, 78, 109

D

Dangote Foundation, 207

E

Eastern Cape Province, 178

Eastern Kentucky University, 162

Electoral Commission of Zambia, 88, 91

European Development Fund, 124

G

GfK Global, 205
Ghana, 53, 148
Gondwe, Michael, 97

H

Hichilema, Hakainde, 18, 30, 66, 74, 75, 76, 216

I

Indian Parliament, 52
Industrial Development Corporation, 101, 102
Innocence Project, 159
Inter-American Development Bank, 49
International Labour Organization, 179

K

Kabimba, Wynter, 66, 133
Kabulonga schools, 209, 210, 211, 213
Kagame, Paul, 144, 148
Kalambo Gorge, 204
Kalingalinga settlement, 217
Kalula, Evance, 234
Kanyama Township, 213
Kapita, Ben, 35
Kappeler, Victor E., 162
Kapwepwe, Simon, 103
Kaseba, Christine, 60
Kaunda, Kenneth, xi, xiii, xiv, 18, 21, 34, 57, 58, 61, 69, 70, 99, 100, 101, 102, 103, 104, 105, 113, 114, 115, 118, 128, 137, 149, 240, 241

Keep Zambia Clean and Healthy, 190
Keep Zambia Clean and Healthy campaign, 189
Konkola Copper Mines Plc, 121
Kwacha, 91, 92, 97, 98, 136, 188, 217
Kyambalesa, Henry, 95

L

Law Association of Zambia, 90, 91
Lima Party, 35
Livingstone Railway Museum, 201, 202
London Court of International Arbitration, 117, 119
Lukoil International Trading and Supply Company, 119
Lumbwe, Kayi, 49
Lungu, Edgar, 26, 29, 31, 36, 51, 66, 71, 91, 134, 135, 141, 145, 146, 150, 182, 229, 242, 243
Luo, Nkandu, 71
Lusaka, 23, 33, 45, 50, 57, 66, 73, 85, 87, 88, 93, 99, 106, 107, 115, 116, 119, 125, 129, 130, 132, 133, 141, 149, 167, 172, 173, 177, 179, 185, 186, 187, 188, 190, 192, 195, 205, 206, 207, 208, 209, 210, 213, 214, 217, 226, 229, 230, 236, 238, 240

M

MacLean, Donald, 48
Mahtani, Rajan, 109, 110, 111, 112, 113, 114, 115, 116, 117, 118, 119, 120, 121, 122, 123, 124, 125, 126, 127, 128, 139, 140
MI-6, 48, 49
Ministry of Home Affairs, 43

Ministry of Overseas Indian Affairs, 52
Movement for Multiparty Democracy, xiii, 19, 28, 99, 105, 172
Mpongwe Development Company, 34
Mukanga, Yamfwa, 140
Mumba, Nevers, 28, 90
Mundia, Nalumino, 103
Mung'omba, Willa, 22, 23, 25, 31, 41, 44, 47
Murtala Muhammed Specialist Hospital in Kano, 208
Mutale, Bonaventure, 117
Mvunga, Patrick, 18, 19
Mwaanga, Vernon, 43, 172
Mwanakatwe, John Mupanga, 19, 20, 21, 22, 104
Mwanawasa, Levy Patrick, xi, 21, 105, 118
National Assembly, 33, 69, 87, 95, 96, 147, 153, 154

N

National Constitutional Conference, 23, 146
National Marketing Board, 34
National Prosecution Authority, 154, 155, 156
National Restoration Party, 24, 64, 152
National Road Fund Agency, 141
National Union of Engineering, Construction and General Workers, 130
Ndola, 62, 74, 76, 109, 112, 114, 118, 119, 131, 179, 183, 184, 188, 211, 229
NGO Coordinating Council of Zambia., 237

Nigerian Centenary Charity Ball, 207
Nixon, Richard, 160
North Atlantic Treaty Organisation, 48

O

Obama, Barack, 77, 78, 160, 161
Office of the Ombudsman, 145, 146
One Party Participatory Democracy', 39
Organization for Economic Co-operation and Development, 143

P

Patriotic Front, xi, 17, 18, 23, 33, 35, 75, 80, 90, 237
Philby, Kim, 48, 49
Phiri, Reggie, 69, 107, 214
Policy Monitoring and Research Centre, 50
Power Africa Innovation Fair, 77
Prison Policy Initiative, 161

Q

Qaddafi, Muammar, 132

R

Road Development Agency, 139, 141, 151
Robert Kapasa Makasa University of Science and Technology, 230, 232
Roberts Construction, 130

S

Sardanis, Andrew, 35, 122, 123
Scott, Guy, 33, 34, 35, 36, 62, 66, 174, 216, 242, 243
Shamabanse, Henry, 135, 136, 137, 149
Simbyakula, Ngosa, 69, 87
Sishuwa, Sishuwa D, 102
Sokoni, Malama, 103, 104, 145, 146
Solar dryers, 196
South Africa, 59, 60, 98, 117, 148, 178, 188, 204, 206, 210, 215
Southern Africa, 203, 206
Southern Province African Farming Improvement Fund, 136

T

Tambo District, 178
Third Republic, 18
Transparency International Zambia, 131, 150, 225
Traore, Karim, ii

U

UN Economic Commission for Africa, 144
United Kingdom, 33, 43, 44, 46, 89, 94, 103, 130, 201, 207, 208, 210, 236
United National Independence Party, xiii, 18, 28, 60

United Nations Entity for Gender Equality and the Empowerment of Women, 234
United Nations World Tourism conference, 200
United Party for National Development, 18, 24, 28, 216
University of Zambia, 188, 231, 232, 233, 237, 238

V

Vedanta Resources Plc, 122
Vera Institute of Justice, 160

W

Washington, 29, 48, 97
World Bank, 35, 86, 94, 142
World University Rankings, 233
World War II, 48

Z

Zambezi Oil and Transport Company, 119
Zambezi Portland Cement, 124
Zambia National Broadcasting Corporation, 240
Zambian Diaspora, 49, 50
Zambians in the Diaspora, 49, 50
Zamtrop, 132

www.ingramcontent.com/pod-product-compliance
Lightning Source LLC
Chambersburg PA
CBHW070401270326
41926CB00014B/2654